The Healer's Calling

*A Spirituality for Physicians and
Other Health Care Professionals*

Daniel P. Sulmasy, O.F.M., M.D.

PAULIST PRESS
New York / Mahwah, N.J.

Cover design by Cindy Dunne.

The Publisher gratefully acknowledges use of the following: Excerpts from "East Coker" and "The Dry Salvages" in *Four Quartets,* T. S. Eliot (Harcourt Brace & Company: Orlando, 1968). Excerpts from "The Love Song of J. Alfred Prufrock," "The Waste Land," and "Ash Wednesday" in *Collected Poems,* T. S. Eliot (Harcourt Brace & Company: Orando, 1963). Excerpt from *The Tao Te Ching No. 71,* by Lao Tsu (Vintage Brooks: New York, 1972). Excerpt from *Personae* by Ezra Pound (New Directions: New York, 1926). Excerpt from *Extravagaria* by Pablo Neruda (Jonathan Cape: London, 1972).

Library of Congress Cataloging-in-Publication Data

Sulmasy, Daniel P., 1956–
   The healer's calling : a spirituality for physicians and other health care professionals / Daniel P. Sulmasy.
     p. cm.
   Includes bibliographical references.
   ISBN 0-8091-3729-1 (alk. paper)
   1. Physicians—Religious life. 2. Medical personnel—Religious life. 3. Christian life—Catholic authors. I. Title.
BV4596.P5S85 1997
248.8′8—dc21
                                                97-20398
                                                 CIP

Published by Paulist Press
997 Macarthur Boulevard
Mahwah, New Jersey 07430

Printed and bound in the
United States of America

CONTENTS

For my novice master,
Rev. Joseph Doino, O.F.M. (1923-1994)

Introduction

This book has grown out of a retreat for physicians that I conducted in Canton, Ohio, in January 1996. It was a moving experience for me. I was profoundly impressed both by the faith of those who attended and by the depth of their spiritual concerns. I reflected that it was remarkable that although I had been engaged in health care ministry for quite a few years as a Franciscan friar, performing one of the ancient "corporal works of mercy," I had never before had a chance to share my spiritual reflections on this work with my colleagues in any extended manner. To be sure, I had given a talk here or there on spirituality and medicine, but these had been largely in secular settings, not in the context of a shared faith. And I had never before had the challenge of organizing such reflections into a thematic series. In preparing for that series of talks, and in the subsequent months, this book has emerged.

This is not a book *about* spirituality in health care. It is a book *of* spirituality in health care. What I mean by this is that the reflections contained herein have arisen out of my own personal experience of being a man of faith engaged in the work of a health care professional. My approach has not been to study spirituality as an abstract subject or to report on surveys of physicians, nurses, and other health care professionals or of patients. My training in philosophy and health services research would allow me to do both, but I am striving after something quite different. This book should be understood as a series of reflections on the lived spiritual experience of one Christian health care professional, asking where God is to be found in the work of health care, and asking where a person who purports to be a follower of Jesus of Nazareth can lay claim to the work of health care in the name of the kingdom of God. It is also an attempt to take seriously the mandate of the Second Vatican Council that the vocation of the laity is to transform the world in the light of the gospel. It is an attempt to ask how this transformation might begin for those whose daily work is with the sick and injured.

There is a hunger for things spiritual in our world today. This hunger is felt very deeply by physicians, nurses, pastoral care staff, medical social workers, and other health care professionals. This yearning for God and for the things of God has arisen at a time when health care is undergoing enormous changes. Many are perplexed, searching for direction in the setting of mergers, layoffs, pressures to control costs, managed care organizations, integrated delivery networks, the closing of public hospitals, and increasing numbers of uninsured and underinsured patients. They want to reclaim the most fundamental meaning of their work in the face of profound confusion.

No matter what kind of health care system we encounter, all of us, whether health care professionals or patients, know that our pilgrimage on this earth ineluctably includes the experiences of illness, injury, and death. We need to know where God is to be found in the experiences both of being ill and of being healers. And so, although this book has been written primarily for health care professionals, anyone who has ever been sick or ever will be sick (which is everyone), is also invited to read. Anyone who is interested in exploring what the encounter between a patient and a health care professional might mean from the viewpoint of faith may at least find in these pages a point of departure for his or her own reflections.

We all have one ultimate destination. Like the pilgrims in Chaucer's *Canterbury Tales*, I invite those who would read this book to join me on a spiritual journey:

> ...to Canterbury they wende
> The holy, blisful martyr for to seeke,
> That hem hath holpen whan that they were seke.

August 1996
Washington, D.C.

Chapter 1

Spirituality and the
Health Care Professional

Longing

There is a deep hunger for things spiritual in our society today. There are signs of it everywhere. It manifests itself in bookstores, movies, yoga classes, self-help groups, and health food stores. Much of this interest is expressed in an eclectic manner. It is probably safe to say that every health care professional has a friend, an acquaintance, or a patient who has become a vegetarian, not for reasons of health, but as a matter of spiritual discipline. Crystals are popular. There is an interest in Eastern religion and in Western chant. It is as if, having thrown off its religious garments in a convulsive fit, Western society is now rummaging around in an antique clothing store, looking for something new to wear.

One might ask oneself why this is happening. Is Freud right in saying that this is all a manifestation of social neurosis?[1] Is it because of worries about the present economic situation in which profits are increasing dramatically for the few while anxiety and insecurity abound for the many, even the middle class? Do people fear that the so-called new world order is rapidly becoming a new world *dis*order? Or are people turning to spirituality because of the stressful pace of modern urban living in which it is now a social sin not to check one's e-mail five times a day?

Perhaps this interest in spirituality is a reaction to a sense of meaninglessness. Many more people today seem to have the sense that life has lost its purpose and direction. There is a gnawing feeling out there that high-minded humanism is not enough.

Or perhaps people are rediscovering the spiritual because there is an uneasy sense that we now occupy a moral vacuum, that we no longer even have a direction in which to set off in search of an answer to our most pressing moral questions. Or perhaps people sense that they have become prisoners of their own technological prowess and that there are no technological solutions to the problems that technology has engendered.

For whatever the reasons, it is simply a fact that people who live in this society today are manifesting a new interest in things spiritual. And this is no less true of physicians and nurses.

Why Toil for What Fails to Satisfy?

Health care professionals are now confronting a curious paradox. While medicine is becoming capable of doing more and more for patients, health care professionals are becoming less and less satisfied with their work. I hardly need to convince anyone that physicians and nurses, as a rule, work extremely hard. Yet the same spiritual hungers that are affecting the rest of society are affecting health care professionals as well. Hard work alone, even for a good cause, is not a spirituality.

The prophet Isaiah asks a question that many health care professionals seem to be asking themselves these days: "Why spend your money for what is not bread; your wages for what fails to satisfy?" (Is. 55:2) Why do physicians and nurses work so hard and yet seem so dissatisfied?

These are indeed hard times for health care professionals. An ancient Chinese curse says, "May you live in an age of transition." Health care represents 15 percent of the economy, so 15 percent of America is in utter turmoil. Health care professionals used to be awash in abbreviations and acronyms of their own creation: COPD, MI, PT/PTT, CMV, WNL, CBC, and so forth. Now they are drowning in a new set of abbreviations created by others: HMO, PPO, IPA, RBRVS, PPRC, HCFA, and so forth. Specialists are being made into generalists. Generalists are being made into gatekeepers. Hospitals are closing. Practices are being bought. Report cards are being issued. Utilization reviewers scrutinize clinical decisions from a thousand miles away.

And our society has also become incredibly litigious. Few physicians can boast any longer that they have never been sued. Physicians, nurses, and physicians' assistants practice "stranger medicine," caring for people they have never met before and will never see again, putting them into the hospital through the MRI-scanner and out through the rehabilitation suite.

All this falls upon a group of allied professions already groaning under the increasingly heavy weight of ethical decision making. Should the patient be put on a ventilator? Should tube feedings be stopped? What do I say when the patient asks me for help committing suicide?

And popular esteem for health care professionals, especially physicians, is also diminishing. Doctors have been knocked off their pedestals. The work is getting harder, and the patients are showing less affection.

Does the question from Isaiah not ring true? Why toil for what fails to satisfy?

Why put up with any of the hassles in order to become a physician or a nurse today?

No sane person would enter medicine in order to make a lot of money and own a big house. I doubt that any house, however large or beautiful, would ever satisfy his or her deepest longings. No sane person would ever enter medicine for the chance to take long vacations. In fact, that's a luxury few physicians actually get. And if they were to get long vacations, wouldn't it be just a bit ironic to say that they work extraordinarily hard in order not to work sometimes? This reasoning is as curious as that of the runner who says that she runs because it feels so good when she stops. No sane person would become a health care professional and work so hard just for the prestige, or for membership in societies, or for more plaques on the wall, or even for the recognition of others. One might reflect for a moment on the plaques that hang on physicians' walls. They all have them. They can be proud of having earned them. But do they mean anything in themselves? Does anyone think that they are enough to keep a physician going, day in and day out? Do plaques satisfy those deepest of human longings?

Some might suggest that technical excellence and successes will be enough to satisfy health care professionals. But I do not believe that this could be true. It is not enough for a surgeon to say that she has cut the correct fascial planes and tied the proper knots. The writing of the correct orders and the cure of pneumococcal pneumonia is not enough to satisfy an internist. The successful angioplasty of another ragged atherosclerotic plaque in the left anterior descending coronary artery is not enough to satisfy a cardiologist. These are all good things, certainly. Health care professionals can be proud of these things and rejoice in them, but they are not enough. It is not enough to live for one's craft alone.

Isaiah's question may touch a nerve. A health care professional will certainly have engaged Isaiah's question if he or she has ever come home at night, angry and frustrated and ready to tell son and daughter alike that they should never go into medicine or nursing or any health care field. Such statements are really just another way of asking Isaiah's question: Why toil for what fails to satisfy?

But if one's longings are for more than possessions or prestige or power or professional expertise, if nothing I have mentioned thus far is enough to satisfy one's longings, then those longings are probably spiritual. And such a conclusion would only be human.

Onions

At the outset, I want to say that I am going to be very specific about what I take spirituality to be. I don't mean to alienate any potential reader. That anyone would take up a book like this and begin to leaf through it, even with idle curiosity, is not be dismissed lightly. I want to invite everyone who takes up this book to develop his or her spiritual life to the fullest.

But it serves no one well if the understanding of spirituality set down in this book is so broad that just about anything imaginable can be considered spirituality. I sense the hunger for spirituality. But I want to invite everyone to a feast that I know is in store for all people. I do not want to leave readers only scraps from the banquet table of the spiritual life (Lk. 16:21).

For all the talk about spirituality in our society today, I suspect that very few people could define it. I want to suggest to you that spirituality is no more and no less than this: very simply put, *one's spirituality is a description of one's relationship with God.* Ultimately, it is only God who can satisfy our deepest desires. Our jobs won't, unless we somehow understand our jobs in relationship to God. Our spouses and families won't, unless our desires for our spouses and families are seen in relationship to God. And quite bluntly, even our church won't, unless our church understands itself in relationship to God. As the psalmist says, "You open wide your hand and satisfy the desire of every living thing" (Ps. 145:16).

Now then, if spirituality is a description of our relationship to God, what is one to make of those many persons today who say, "I don't believe in God, but I'm a very spiritual person"? This probably has a familiar ring to it. Perhaps some readers have heard themselves utter such a sentence or think such a thought. Would such persons be correct in concluding that I will have nothing to say to them or that I am unnecessarily excluding them? I don't believe so for a minute.

Anyone who says, "I don't believe in God, but I'm a very spiritual person" is obviously offering a reflection about something he or she has experienced. And since they are calling it spirituality, I suspect that they are talking about an experience of something other than themselves. So it is an experience of something or other that is either outside them or inside them but not equivalent to them. And unless they think that they were hallucinating, it follows logically that such persons will also believe that whatever it is that is giving rise to their experiences must exist.

Now, it may be the case that they simply refuse to call whatever it is that they are experiencing by the name "God," even though they might believe that the source of this experience has all the characteristics of what some of the rest of us call God. The character Mitsuko in Shusaku Endo's novel, *Deep River,*[2] for example, refuses to use the word *God,* and she tells the awkward young Catholic man whom she successfully seduces for the fun of it that she is very curious about why he prays to his "Onion." Mitsuko, it turns out, is a very spiritual person on a journey of her own. But she refuses to name what she experiences "God."

For others, it is a bit more complex. Logic requires that they believe that whatever it is that gives rise to their spiritual experiences exists. But they either deny or have doubts about whether this "Onion" has any of the other characteristics that some of the rest of us might attribute to it, such as being a Creator, being all-loving, being the source of moral guidance, or having become human in the person of Jesus Christ. Nonetheless, I can talk meaningfully about spirituality with such people. If they affirm the experience and believe that it has a source, then we might not give it the same name or believe exactly the same things about the nature of the source of spiritual experience, but we will share the belief that we have a relationship with it, whatever it is. Even the atheist who denies not only God, but spiritual experience as well, still has a relationship with both, at least as propositions to be denied.[3]

So those readers who might not believe in God but have a hunger for the spiritual and believe that you have a relationship to the spiritual will pardon me if I call the source of our mutual experiences "God." If one prefers "Onion" or some other name, feel free to translate. I believe that I have far too much in common with anyone who considers himself or herself a "spiritual" person to miss the opportunity for dialogue.

Trusting in Spiritual Experience

That Holy Other with which all spiritual persons are in relationship (that which I call God), is nothing other than that which satisfies the deepest longings of the human race. The spiritual relationship is a relationship of love—love beyond all telling. Spiritual experience is the experience of God's transcendent love, God's overwhelming and universal concern for every single human being.

As a relationship of love, however, genuine spirituality also makes demands of us. Genuine spirituality cannot be a one-way street. While God is the one who satisfies the deepest of human longings, spirituality is not only about good feelings. It is not only about shelter from the storm of upheaval in the world of health care. It is not only about feelings of peace. It *is* all these things, but if it is *only* these things it is not genuine spirituality. Genuine spirituality will make demands of anyone who takes it seriously. It will make one take risks. It will ask one to make sacrifices. It will ask for love.

Anyone who experiences this deep spiritual longing and finds that there *is* a Something out there that is tugging at the heart, tugging at the soul, calling out from above and whispering from within, has a choice. A person can either give himself or herself over to that experience, or withdraw from it. My advice is to do more than merely flirt.

Surrender to the Voice that calls you. Trust in it. Give it a name. Let it love you. Let it make demands of you.

The widespread interest in things spiritual that is all around in contemporary popular culture is at once gratifying and sad. So many people are hearing God's message of love. But for so very many it remains unconsummated. As the poet, T.S. Eliot, has put it, "We had the experience, but missed the meaning."[4] I am really talking about what faith means at its very core. Faith is primarily about trust in God and only secondarily about an affirmation of credal propositions.

Spirituality is a relationship of love. And like any other relationship of love, spirituality takes time to develop. It waxes and wanes. It can grow warm, and it can grow cold. It is a relationship that is sometimes in need of healing and forgiveness. It requires commitment despite day in and day out drudgery. It needs time alone for intimate sharing. It needs attention. It requires work.

Far too much of what passes for spirituality today is a form of either drug abuse or narcissism. Spirituality cannot be just another species of the consumerism of experience, trying to get "high" through meditation or to find feelings of peace mediated though a crystal. These will not ultimately satisfy. They may dull the pains of practice for a while, but they will wear off like the intoxication of whisky and leave one with a bad hangover in the morning. And the utilization reviewers will still remain every bit as annoying the day after as they did the day before.

Go, instead, after God, who opens wide his hand and satisfies the desire of every living thing. Go for love, not cheap substitutes. Reach for the transcendent. Find it in the pedestrian. Seek first the kingdom of God, and all else will follow (Mt. 6:33).

Healing and Magic

So how does a physician, a nurse, or any other health care professional begin to figure out how to respond to the love of God, once he or she has recognized it? I think that for a Christian, the best way to begin is by asking how Jesus, the Great Physician, went about his work. We can probably learn a lot from the scriptures, in which Jesus is described over and over again in acts of healing.

One of the friars in my community once confessed in a homily that while he was in grade school, he had asked Sr. Mary McGillicuddy, his fourth grade teacher, why Jesus hadn't just cured everyone in the world once and for all. Why just a few isolated miracles? After all, he was God. And as every fourth grader knows, there are lots of sick people in the world in need of cure.

Not a bad question for a fourth grader. Perhaps it is a question that health care professionals sometimes ask themselves. Perhaps it is a question that their patients put, in one form or another, to their chaplains and to their pastors.

I will not pretend to develop a theodicy or a theological explanation of the problem of the existence of evil in a world created by an all-loving God. Those who are interested in this topic can find it addressed in other books (plenty have been written). What I *am* interested in is the relationship between the fact of the physical evils of sickness and dying, spirituality, and the work of the health care professional.

I think that the key to understanding this relationship lies in the difference between magic and healing. Jesus was no magician. Jesus was, and continues to be, a healer. Magic is a zap from the sky, but healing is a deeply human process. Magic is impersonal, but healing involves intimacy and relationships. True healing takes place only when the healer is related to the one who is healed—through, in, and with a relationship to the transcendent.

Jesus is the preeminent healer precisely because he is constitutively in relationship with the transcendence of the Father and because to be a person in relationship with Jesus, standing before Jesus as one in need of his healing, is to be in relationship with the transcendent.

No physician or nurse is Jesus. But health care professionals can cultivate their own relationships with Jesus and live in connection with their Savior. That is what it means for any Christian to be spiritual.

In truth, no physician or nurse is a magician. But they can be, and have pledged themselves to be, healers. Health care professionals can only be healers like Jesus the healer if they are in right relationship not only with God, but also with their patients. The healing work in which they are engaged is deeply human. It is not magic.

The story of Simon Magus from the Acts of the Apostles (8:9–25) is very instructive. Simon was a magician who passed himself off as important. He saw that the apostles could heal through the Holy Spirit, having been granted the authority to do so by Christ. He became a convert and then asked the apostles whether he could purchase the power of the Spirit from them. Simon Magus earned a sharp rebuke from Peter, but after that, he recognized the error of his ways and reformed his life.

Simon Magus thought healing was magic. He thought it happened outside of the context of truly personal relationships between human beings and their personal relationships with the transcendent.[5] But he was no healer. He was only a magician. Physicians and nurses are at their very worst when they think they are magicians.

Warfield T. Longcope, the third Professor of Medicine at the Johns Hopkins University School of Medicine, once wrote that, "even though a clinician has science, art, and craftsmanship, unless he is intensely interested in human beings, he is not likely to be a good doctor."[6]

This is why even the doctor who diligently works on the perfection of his or her craft will never ultimately be satisfied by technical excellence alone. Technical competence is necessary, but it is insufficient for healing. Healing requires a recognition of the human face of each person one sets out to heal and a communication of the message that both the healer and the healed share a bond that ties them to each other through their humanity, their mortality, and the God-given spark of grace that lives in each of them.

Jesus the Physician

The first chapter of the gospel of Mark is instructive for health care professionals. One might even consider it the original and only certainly valid set of practice guidelines one will ever need.

In this chapter, after his baptism, Jesus goes off into the desert to pray. He is tempted there, perhaps as any health care professional might sometimes be, to give up in the face of adversity, turmoil, confusion, misunderstanding, and hassle. But with the help of his Father, he rejects the temptation to cynicism and despair and finds courage and strength in his relationship with the Father. It is then that he begins to proclaim the good news.

His first healing is cited in Mark 1:23 and following. A man convulsed by demons appears before him. Jesus asks no questions, wastes no time. He heals with the authority granted to him by God.

Word gets around. His practice attracts attention. Immediately thereafter, he is called to the bedside of Peter's mother-in-law. The description of his encounter with her is compellingly human. Scripture says that "He went over to her and grasped her hand and helped her up, and the fever left her. She immediately began to wait on them." (v. 31).

His clinical reputation grows. His practice builds up. He even starts, it seems, to keep evening office hours. "When it was evening, after sunset, they brought to him all who were ill or possessed by demons. The whole town was gathered at the door. He cured many who were sick with various diseases..."(vv. 32–34).

These passages from the gospel of Mark depict deeply human encounters. The people who came to Jesus were no different, I am sure, than those with various afflictions who come to doctors' offices, emergency rooms, and hospitals today. Jesus healed them because he loved them. And health care professionals can learn to do likewise.

But Mark's gospel has more to tell physicians and nurses. Continuing in the first chapter, Mark tells us that Jesus went off again to pray. "Rising very early before dawn, he left and went off to a deserted place, where he prayed" (v. 35). For the health care professional, love for one's patients alone will not ultimately satisfy. Patients can be very fickle. They can bring frivolous lawsuits against those who did their best in love to help them, and this can be deeply hurtful. Patients can be demanding at times. They can be ungrateful at times. The relationship to the patient will not be a full healing relationship if one cannot see it in the context of one's relationship with God—one's spirituality. If a health care professional is not careful to cultivate a spiritual life, he or she will quickly end up becoming cynical about patients. No physician or nurse will last very long in health care looking to patients themselves for personal satisfaction. Patients can only be the point of departure. They are not the source of satisfaction, but signposts that point the way to satisfaction. Physicians and nurses are really doing their jobs when they see each patient as a precious being swept up into the mystery of God's love. God is the destination.

Still in the first chapter of Mark, after Jesus has completed his desert retreat, a leper approaches him, asking to be cured. The encounter is described in even more fully human terms. Jesus, the fullness of the transcendent love of God present in our human frame, is stirred with compassion. The text says, "Moved with pity, Jesus stretched out his hand, touched him, and said, 'I do will it. Be made clean'" (v. 41).

All the elements Jesus had at his disposal are at the disposal of health care professionals today as well. Jesus had compassion for this sick human being, he touched him, and he spoke to him. As Jesus did, so doctors and nurses are called to do. No matter how sophisticated the technology of healing gets, true healing will involve these three very simple human elements: compassion, touch, and conversation. Jesus was moved with pity. Jesus touched the leper. Jesus spoke words of healing and comfort. And so can anyone who practices the healing arts today. If one can learn how to place these elements at the service of one's patients, with whom one is in right relationships of love in and through one's relationship with God from whom all healing and all love flows, one can become a true healer.

To remind Christian health care professionals again of how all this can be accomplished, the first chapter of the gospel of Mark ends with Jesus once again retiring to "desert places" (v. 45).

Transcendent healing is what everyone hungers for. *This* is what will satisfy. *This* is what will sustain physicians and nurses through the troubled times that the health care enterprise is facing. Physicians and nurses can be truly spiritual men and women. Physicians and nurses can learn to see their patients as sacraments—doorways into the sacred. Physicians and nurses also need to take time away from patients to be alone with God, to rediscover in prayer, who they are in an authentic way, and to discover, perhaps for the first time, who their patients really are.

Health care is a supremely human enterprise. It is also divine. God comes to health care professionals daily as the one true source of all the healing with which they are so busily engaged. At the same time, God comes to doctors and nurses as the One who stands before them naked, in need of the healing powers that have been given to them. If they fail to recognize God in their midst, health care will lose its soul.

God comes into the midst of health care with all the immediacy of human encounters. As the scripture says, "The leprosy left him immediately, and he was made clean" (v. 42). God's presence in the clinical encounter is truly a matter of then and there, now and here. It is not magic. It is not a sparkling wand waved over the world by a distant God. God is in the healing, and the healing is in our relationship with God.

Remember Your Journey's Beginning

I hope that in the pages of this book I can stimulate some thinking about where the reader may be going in his or her own spiritual journey. Although others may read these words, I want, in particular, to walk with my fellow health care professionals on their spiritual journeys.

To figure out where one is going, it sometimes helps to think about where one started. It is extraordinarily common for applicants to medical school to be asked during interviews why they want to be doctors. But curiously, after that, it seems that no one again either asks or seems to care. I make a point of explaining this to the residency applicants that I interview. I ask them what they said in response to this question when interviewing for medical school, what they would say now, and how the two answers compare. I could ask the same set of questions of all physicians, nurses, or other health care professionals practicing today. The results might be very interesting.

I am firmly convinced that if health care professionals could just lay hold of what got them started in the first place—the original zeal, now sobered but still maturely passionate, the interest in other human beings, the desire to put their talents to use for the service of others—health care would be much the better for it.

A career in health care can be a spiritual journey. It can lead to holiness just as naturally and with just as much difficulty as the life of any monk or nun. And wise spiritual writers know the value of setting the course of a spiritual journey right again by examining how it all got started. Hear, then, the words of St. Clare to Blessed Agnes of Prague:

> ...always remember your resolution,
> And be conscious of how you began.
> What you hold, may you always hold.
> What you do, may you always do, and never abandon.
> But with swift pace, and light step, and unswerving feet,
> So that even your steps stir no dust,
> Go forward securely, joyfully, and swiftly
> On the path of wisdom and happiness...[7]

Over the course of this book, I will be talking about healing and compassion and prayer and lepers and doctors and patients. But through it all, I will be challenging the reader to think about his or her own relationship with God—that is, spirituality. I take the fact that the reader has opened the pages of a book on this subject as a sign of concern about a personal relationship with God. But that relationship cannot be cultivated merely by my writing. Health professionals need to take time alone with God in quiet.

Be sure to take advantage of the opportunities that may come your way. Do not let your spirit be made numb by medicine. Do not allow bureaucratic or economic or academic pursuits to keep you from God. If this book thwarts, rather than facilitates, the cultivation of your relationship with God, throw it away. Remember your journey's beginning. Take a walk with God. Read the scriptures and listen to what God has to say to you. I simply pray that I may be able in some small way to help you along in your spiritual journey. In return, I ask only for your prayers for me in my own relationship with God.

Chapter 2

Medicine, Love, and the Art of Being Uncertain

T. S. Eliot's poem, "The Love Song of J. Alfred Prufrock," has more to say about the current problems facing medicine than we care to imagine.[1] Prufrock is the archetypal twentieth-century Westerner, and American physicians embody the twentieth-century Westerner in a most exemplary fashion. All too often, physicians seem to walk down the halls of hospitals toward their patients, hoping to find them "etherized upon a table." Like poor J. Alfred, it is their demand for rock-bottom proof ("proof-rock") before undertaking any definitive action that is largely responsible for the undoing of medicine. Health care professionals are gradually becoming paralyzed by their inability to tolerate uncertainty. As Prufrock would not dare to eat a peach for fear that his dentures might fall out, so physicians and other health care professionals do not dare to tell their patients, "I don't know."

Fear of Uncertainty

Physicians today are so afraid of uncertainty that they fear being generalists (how can one possibly know everything about everything); they fear the consequences of not doing CT scans for headaches (after all, it might be a tumor); they fear not doing PSA screening tests for prostate cancer (after all, the patient might sue if he gets cancer).

> "Is it perfume from a dress
> That makes me so digress?
> . . . .
[What]
> If one, settling a pillow or throwing off a shawl,
> And turning toward the window, should say:
>   "That is not it at all;
>   That is not what I meant, at all."
. . . .

23

This profound intolerance for uncertainty that characterizes our culture is certainly something health care professionals share with their patients.

For example, some advocate that since prostate cancer grows very slowly and since most men who develop prostate cancer die of something else, patients who have an elevated Prostate Specific Antigen (PSA) level on screening may want to consider postponing surgery for prostate cancer until it declares itself to be a problem. This strategy is called "watchful waiting." But patients do not seem very tolerant of this uncertainty. Most report that this would make them anxious.[2] Of course, the mutual intolerance for uncertainty that health care professionals share with their patients has also made many people wealthy. And the manufacturers of the latest scanners and the biotech companies hope that it will continue to make them wealthy as well.

This intolerance for uncertainty affects all spheres of medical care, not just test ordering. A bioethicist I know describes the importance of advance directives (such as living wills and durable powers of attorney for health care) in terms of the patient's interest in his or her own *life plan*. Planning will overcome our uncertainties, or so some people think. So dominant a feature is the concept of a life plan in this bioethicist's writings that it has almost become his equivalent of the Cartesian *Cogito, ergo sum*. In this bioethicists's world view, "I plan, therefore I am."

The profound reach of this intolerance for uncertainty came home to me a few years ago when we had an afternoon off at a bioethics retreat during which we set out on a whitewater rafting trip. This in itself was a comic sight—fifty out-of-shape bioethicists in sunscreen and wet sneakers preparing for a whitewater rafting trip! In the midst of this amusing scene, I told the bioethicist to whom I referred above a story about an appearance on the Johnny Carson show by the poet James Dickey. Dickey, you will recall, wrote the novel *Deliverance*.[3] Carson asked Dickey if he actually did things like whitewater canoeing. Dickey replied that he did and that he was also an avid parachute jumper. Carson then inquired whether Dickey thought this was a good idea, given his status as a husband and father, a professor, and a renowned writer. After all, weren't these practices a bit too risky?

Dickey replied, "John, comes a time in a man's life when the only sane thing he can do with it is to risk it."

I find this story both amusing and instructive. What I found most amazing was that my bioethicist colleague didn't get it. He looked at me as if I had just told him that I had seen invaders from Mars. There did not seem to be space in his worldview for the sentiment that would drive T.S. Eliot to extol, as he did in *The Wasteland,* "The awful daring of a moment's surrender. Which an age of prudence can never retract."[4] Life, for this bioethicist, like so many health care professionals, seemed to consist of the dreary hebetude of avoiding uncertainties and risks. Never mind, in addition, the fact that such a life would be impossible to achieve. I plan, therefore I am.

There was a small flurry of literature on the topic of uncertainty in the medical journals about a decade ago, but it has largely died down. This group of scholars advocated tolerance for uncertainty as a way to reduce excessive testing. They advocated shared uncertainty between clinicians and patients as a way to reduce malpractice claims. They advocated tolerance for uncertainty as a way to practice more rational medicine. I imagine that few, if any, were granted tenure. One no longer hears much about this topic. The NIH, General Electric, and drug companies apparently don't give research grants to help health care professionals tolerate uncertainty.

Uncertain Judgments

Now what kind of uncertainty am I talking about? And what kind of tolerance for uncertainty am I advocating?

First, let me make it clear that I am advocating neither blissful ignorance nor a spirit of recklessness. It is a good thing to be able to have some ability to predict and to control the future. But like most good things, if carried to an extreme it becomes a vice. I am urging an Aristotelian mean. Too strong a commitment to the reduction of uncertainty is just as bad as *never* looking ahead and *never* planning.

Second, I am not talking about the difference between classical and statistical knowledge. I am talking about uncertainty in *judgment,* not probability.

It is good for health care professionals, continually blitzed with statistics, to try to understand the difference between statements of the sort, "the probability is x," and statements of the sort, "this is probably true." The sense of probability invoked in each statement is different. When one reads that the prevalence of a disease in a certain population is 25 percent, this probability is a frequency. It is a statement of fact, like "the sky is blue." The only difference is that the frequency is describing a nonsystematic fact. But as a statement of fact, it can either be true or false, likely or unlikely.

A judgment that something is true or false is rarely made with certitude in medicine. Medical judgments are *probable* judgments, and they are made with varying degrees of certainty. When one reads that "the P-value is .05," this means, more or less, that it is 95 percent certain that the probability that anyone in the population described has the specified disease is what one claims it to be (*e.g.*, 25 percent).

I can be more or less certain about my judgments, whether these be scientific judgments about frequencies, or common-sense judgments about what to do for particular patients. For instance, I am only a very, very, very little uncertain about whether the sun will rise tomorrow. I am substantially more uncertain about my judgments regarding statistical knowledge, like tomorrow's weather.

I am perhaps more uncertain about my judgments regarding the prognosis of individual patients. All of these are kinds of knowledge about which my job requires that I make judgments under conditions of uncertainty. Clinicians are most intolerant of the uncertainty that is inherent in the treatment of individual patients and cannot be eliminated.

Examples abound. Clinicians would rather use the antibiotic that kills 99 percent of the bacteria that are likely to be causing an infection, even though it is ten times more expensive than the antibiotic that kills 98 percent of the bacteria. Clinicians obtain "baseline" EKGs and run twenty blood tests on an automated analyzer for healthy 30-year-olds. Clinicians diagnose somatization disorder (psychosomatic illness) only after ruling out every other possible physiological explanation for the patient's symptoms.

Some health care professionals even invoke their uncertainty that their patients will be able to bear up under the stress of frank conversations about life and death issues to justify their own reluctance to talk about questions like whether or not the patient should be resuscitated.

Uncertainty and Faith

What could possibly be the connection, one may ask, between all this talk about uncertainty and the practice of medicine and the spiritual life? The answer is rather simple if one tries to understand what faith is about. As I said in chapter 1, faith has more to do with trust than it does with belief. Religious faith is not primarily intellectual assent to a creed or an exercise in theological justification. Faith is primarily *trust*. To say that one has faith in God is to say that one has *trust* in God. The old Latin was *Credo in unum Deum*. I believe in one God. I don't say, "I believe God," as in "I believe all those crazy things God tells me." I say, I believe *in* God. I put my trust in this person.

J. Alfred Prufrock's fear of rejection by others led him to be very careful about every human interaction. He trusted no one. He lacked the courage of his convictions. In fact, he lacked any convictions.

> Deferential, glad to be of use,
> Politic, cautious, and meticulous;
> Full of high sentence, but a bit obtuse;
> At times, indeed, almost ridiculous—
> Almost, at times, the Fool.
> . . . .

Sadly, there are too many physicians and other health care professionals for whom this is an apt description.

The quest for certainty undermines trust. The quest for certainty fills the vacuum that remains as trust evaporates from the doctor-patient relationship. Intolerance for uncertainty results from the absence of a certain basic trust, informed by a strong belief that the future could not possibly turn out OK for me unless I manipulate things and people in order to *make* it come out OK.

Tolerance for uncertainty, by contrast, demands a level of basic trust. In the present era, however, this trust is hard to come by. It now seems as if doctors no longer trust their patients and patients no longer trust their doctors.

It is not easy to say what accounts for this situation, but I think health care professionals themselves, taken as a whole, are largely to blame. One source of this distrust and intolerance for uncertainty is that medicine has been so successful in convincing the public of its invincible powers and the certainty of a cure for everything, that death and other human limitations on medicine are now interpreted as someone's fault. This is one of the causes of the malpractice explosion and the growth of defensive medicine.

Another source of mistrust is the cynical attitude toward doctors that doctors themselves have cultivated among the public. For instance, patients fail to see how doctors can claim not to see a conflict of interest in owning stock in the drugs they promote or in the devices they investigate in their laboratories. Patients fail to see how physicians can claim to find nothing wrong with physician ownership of free-standing radiation therapy facilities, when it has been shown that physicians who have joint ownership of such facilities refer their patients for radiation therapy more regularly than reasonable medicine would suggest is necessary.[5] Patients fail to see how organized medicine can claim to put patients first when organized medicine has, by and large, fought against every type of true health care reform.

Patients have noticed that instead of advocating for our patients against the abuses in managed care, physicians are now busy trying to find the best ways to cash in on the affair, claiming that things will be better only if doctors own the HMOs. Yet studies demonstrate that when doctors run the HMO, they use the same cost-control techniques and the same distorted financial incentives as those used when the HMO is owned and operated by business professionals who have taken no oath to serve patients.[6] No wonder patients have so little trust in their doctors. And where there is no trust, there can be no room for tolerating uncertainty.

Positivism

Yet the roots of this intolerance for uncertainty among health care professionals go even deeper. For while the basic sciences have begun to move away from a positivistic view of science and of the world in general, such views seem to be deepening their hold on medicine. Positivism is a radically empiricist school of philosophy that holds that nothing exists unless it can be empirically verified.[7] Verification depends (ultimately) on sense data. Knowledge comes to mean having an appearance. I call this "picture thinking," a term borrowed from Wittgenstein.[8]

In physics, this has long been discredited. Mu-mesons are not empirically verifiable. Research in physics now often consists of experiments in which gigabytes of data, all theory-laden and far removed from primary sense observations, are crunched through a computer calculation to give a result. Both the questions and the answers are unpicturable.

But medicine remains obsessed with pictures. The more technologically sophisticated the pictures are, the better. It is instructive to take notice of the appearance of a relatively new feature in the *New England Journal of Medicine* known as "Images in Medicine."[9] This is picture thinking at its finest. What has happened during the short life of this feature section has been intriguing, but also quite telling. It began with a few clinical photos of a few peculiar rashes. That lasted about two weeks.

Now this section is regularly filled with examples of sophisticated imaging techniques—high-tech pictures with flashing lights and dazzling dials and attractive colors. Week in and week out, picture thinking in health care is now slowly being reinforced by that highest of all authorities, the *New England Journal of Medicine*.

Knowledge and Relationships

But real knowledge is about relationships, not images. To know a thing is to grasp what makes it different from other things and how it relates to other things in the knowledge matrix. For example, to know a ratio is to know a relationship between one number and another. To know an irrational number is to know a relationship that is utterly unimaginable and unpicturable.

To know pneumococcal pneumonia is to know a highly interrelated focus of data that is a relationship, doubtless consisting of some picturable things, but really something that is ultimately unpicturable. Pneumococcal pneumonia is not gram positive diplococci under a microscope. It is not a characteristic chest X ray. It is not a cough and rigors. It is a *relationship* between these and other data, as well as a shared understanding between doctor and patient.

Matter itself is probably best conceptualized as a relatively persistent set of relationships in a field. At the subatomic level where matter begins, particles can no longer be thought of as tiny cannonballs dropped from the Tower of Pisa. Field is prior to matter. Particles are wrinkles in the electromagnetic field, of durations that last anywhere from a few nanoseconds to a few centuries. Matter can no longer be thought of as isolated bits of particularity. Substance *is* relationship. Knowledge is the grasp of relationships. And the most important relationships, like the love between a husband and a wife, the love between God and the people of God—and yes, the love between doctors and patients—are unpicturable. One cannot see love under a microscope. One can gain insights into these relationships through pictures, but the pictures are only windows through which one attains the knowledge. Pictures are not the knowledge itself.

We are also at the dawn of the statistical age in medicine. Ultimately, this is the real revolution in medicine, not the molecular revolution. Genes are statistical entities, not pictures. (Ask Brother Gregor Mendel, the great counter of peas.) And statistical knowledge is real knowledge. It is pure relationship. To know a mean is to know something very real. It is to know that value from which a nonsystematic process cannot systematically deviate.[10]

The physicists are way ahead here. What is an orbital but a statistical description of the relationship between an electron and a nucleus? Knowledge is a grasp of relationships, not a picture.

So, the science of medicine has now become the science of relationships understood in terms of probability. And the art of medicine remains what it always has been—the making of judgments and the carrying out of therapeutic actions under conditions of uncertainty in the setting of a relationship of trust. The great Dr. William Osler had it almost right when he said, "Medicine is a science of uncertainty and an art of probability."[11] However, he used his terms too loosely. The correct insight is that "Medicine is a science of probability and an art of uncertainty." Unfortunately, no matter how it is phrased, health care professionals have yet to pay sufficient attention to this insight in their practices.

Spirituality, Relationships, and Trust

So how does this relate to spirituality? Well, it does so in some profound ways. To begin with, for Christians, God's nature is relationship. That is the mystery of the Trinity. And salvation history in the Judeo-Christian tradition is the story of the relationship between God and the people of God. On an individual basis, the believer's life of prayer, whatever his or her religion, is a relationship between God and the praying person. The spiritual person is one who enters into a web of relationships in a spirit of gratitude and trust—relationships between God and the believer, the believer and other people, the believer and all of creation. To know oneself is to grasp a relationship.

The spiritual doctor or nurse or other health care professional is one who enters into relationships of trust with patients: inviting trust, behaving in a trustworthy manner regardless of whether or not that trust is reciprocated, and trusting in the basic goodness of a world of healing relationships. This takes great faith. It is risky. Each and every one of these relationships requires a high tolerance for uncertainty. There is risk and uncertainty in loving patients. The patient may not reciprocate the clinician's trust. The patient might sue. The patient might not get well. The clinician might make a mistake or act in ignorance or meet the limits of medicine. But for the believing, trusting clinician, God is never absent, even from the failures and the frailty of the human. The failure and frailty of the human are the stuff of daily experience.

It takes a lot of humility to trust. But being a good healer demands humility. Humility is one of the virtues that accompanies tolerance for uncertainty. Tolerance for uncertainty is one of the consequences of knowing that one does not know. To admit that one does not know is an expression of humility. As the author of the Tao Te Ching observes, "Knowing ignorance is strength."[12] And this strength is good for patients.

My mentor, Dr. Edmund Pellegrino, says that he really only used to have one line of questioning when he interviewed medical school applicants. No matter what the subject they wanted to talk about, he would keep asking questions until he heard them say, "I don't know." Only then did he think that they had the intellectual integrity to be physicians.

The standards for medical school applicants are generally not Dr. Pellegrino's standards. Most clinicians have met at least one arrogant know-it-all surgeon whose knowledge and skills place her or him above the patient. And most have met at least one supercilious internist who treats patients and other health care professionals with disdain. No one wants to be treated by such physicians. Such surgeons will keep cutting until they get rid of the infection, even as the streptococcal myonecrosis ("flesh eating bacteria") advances up the abdomen before their very eyes. Such internists will keep running tests until they find the answer, damn it. They are not very tolerant of uncertainty. The patient becomes a mere pretext for a display of knowledge and skill. But this is hardly treating the patient as a person.

Tolerance for Uncertainty and Clinical Practice

Tolerance for uncertainty is a good thing, but it has lots of consequences for those who seek it. It requires coming to terms with one's humanity. To be forced to make decisions, to act, and to refrain from action in spite of one's ignorance is part of the human condition. Medical deities do not want to be human.

All medical actions will be fraught with uncertainty if one is honest about it. Yet, as T.S. Eliot says in his essay on Pascal, "The demon of doubt...is inseparable from the spirit of belief."[13] Faithful trust is required in order to act in the face of uncertainty. The strength for such action is spiritual. Consistent, trusting, faithful action in the face of uncertainty and doubt demands other virtues, such as practical wisdom, patience, and courage. The life of virtue is fully human life. Clinicians need to be better at being human if they are to be better clinicians.

As Paul Ramsey once said, "The function of medicine is not to relieve the human condition of the human condition."[14] That lesson is too easily forgotten. Tied to the naive quest for certitude is a naive quest for earthly immortality.

Spirituality, Uncertainty, and Health Care

Where does all this lead one in terms of spirituality and the actual practice of medicine, nursing, and the other health care professions? Several points can be made:

First, good clinicians learn to prioritize decision making over certitude. One will never be absolutely certain about anything one decides in health care. But one will never be effective if one is not decisive. Sometimes the best decision is an action, but sometimes the best decision is inaction, as long as it is *thoughtful* inaction. After all, sometimes it is best in clinical practice to follow the aphorism, "Don't just do something. Stand there!"

Decisions are required in the face of ineluctable uncertainty. Did I do the right thing? is a question one can always ask. But one cannot be a Prufrock, paralyzed by uncertainty. And patients should not be made victims of professional uncertainty. Clinicians are constantly making choices for and with their patients. The problem is that they generally aren't certain which choice is correct. And yet, decisions must be made. Part of the art of clinical medicine is to steer a course between the rash and the indecisive. Finding the right path between the rash and the indecisive, between ordering too many tests and treatments and ordering too few tests and treatments, is not easy. Looking for this balance, being aware of it as a question, honing one's skills, aiming for the ideals of therapeutic parsimony and diagnostic elegance[15] requires spiritual discipline worthy of a Zen master. This is the challenge patients have entrusted to the healing professions.

Second, good clinicians recognize that their practices are part of a great tradition of scientific and artistic knowledge. Lots of people have shared in the uncertainties before, and they have taught today's clinicians lessons in how to act in such circumstances. Biomedical knowledge is part of a network of knowledge that dates back to Hippocrates. One learns in relationship to that network. One can find a basis for rational action through one's connection with that network. It is a network that consists of both classical and statistical scientific knowledge and the cumulative practical wisdom of clinicians. Health care professionals read journals and also ask the advice of good clinicians. One never really practices medicine, nursing, or any other health care profession alone. Even the solo practitioner, that dying breed, is never really solo. He or she is part of a tradition.

Being a health care professional is a bit like being a member of the clergy. For the clergy, there is a scientific store of knowledge known as theology and a practical store of knowledge known as pastoral care. Similarly, the health care professions have both basic science and clinical knowledge bases. The uncertainty becomes easier to deal with once one recognizes that one is not alone.

Third, good clinicians learn to prioritize process over results. This is probably the hardest spiritual challenge in health care. Spirituality, in general, has more to do with process than with results. Perhaps this is why contemporary culture, fanatically oriented towards results, has such a difficult time with spirituality. And all of this is made much harder by the tremendous emphasis on outcomes in medicine today. Contemporary Western society doggedly seeks the certainty of results, not the uncertainties of process.

Let me quote to you from the letters of Thomas Merton. The reader may recognize someone familiar:

> You are probably striving to build yourself an identity in your work...using it, so to speak, to protect yourself against nothingness, annihilation. That is not the right use of your work. All the good that you do will not come from you but from the fact that you have allowed yourself, in the obedience of faith, to be used by God's love...The real hope, then, is not in something we think we can do, but in *God* who is making something good out of it in some way we cannot see...[16]

If one treats HIV-infected heroin addicts and one is in it for the results, one will wind up a bitter person very quickly. When someone's diabetes begins to eat away at their toes and one has dilated and bypassed their femoral arteries twice and the gangrene continues to progress, if one is in it for the results, one will be frustrated. As a patient's Alzheimer's disease progresses and one can't do a darn thing to stop it, if one is in it for the results, one will soon begin to resent the fact that someone brought her to the office in the first place.

Health care, in the final analysis, is not about results. Not that one can ignore the results or that one has no responsibility to try to cure when one can, but health care is primarily about relationships of knowledge, of trust, and of care. Health care is about being there with people in their finitude and doubt, in their pain and uncertainty, respecting each one and saying that one cares, and showing by one's deeds that one really does care in all the ways that one can. Such caring does mean acting in a way that promotes the best results possible. But the results, ultimately, are really Someone Else's business.

Fourth, good clinicians always maintain their orientation toward the truth–in humble recognition of their limited ability to know that truth. Genuine humility will prompt an openness to revision. But this is not the indecisiveness of Prufrock, who sang the refrain:

> And indeed there will be a time
> . . . .
> There will be time, there will be time
> . . . .
> And time yet for a hundred indecisions,
> And for a hundred visions and revisions,
> Before the taking of a toast and tea.
> . . . .

Humility is not indecisiveness, but neither is it bull-headed stubbornness. One must have the inner strength to let go of diagnoses and consider other diagnoses when things aren't going as predicted. The patients that get me into the most trouble are those for whom I profess to be certain of a particular diagnosis and so start forcing the clinical data to fit that diagnosis. The best clinicians are honest with themselves and honest with their patients. The best clinicians are humble, uncertain, and open to revision.

God and Uncertainty

None of this should be taken as a defense of the notion that God is the one who fills in the gaps in our knowledge. I have no need for such a god. My God is the ground of everything I know, the ground of all relationships. My God is not the answer machine. My God is the transcendent presence alive in my practice, alive in my uncertainties. God is alive at that moment when the patient inhales and the subtle tip of a distended spleen touches my knowing fingers and then fades away into the denouement of expiration.

God is the horizon of our expectations, the transcendent presence beyond our mortality, our failure, our limitation, the humanity that is the stuff of our day-to-day medical experience. God is the point of our hope, the context of our care, the source of our courage to reach out in uncertainty to love our patients—to care about them, to care for them, to think about them, to talk to them, to touch them, to heal them, to be with them through sickness and death and even, perhaps, beyond the horizon of the human into eternity. We can be certain of none of this. We can only have faith—faith enough to be healers for people broken in body and in spirit who entrust all their uncertainty to our care.

Chapter 3

The Wine of Fervent Zeal and the Oil of Compassion

The health care professions (such as nursing and medicine) have become increasingly less attractive careers in the waning years of the twentieth century. Nurses are going to business school in record numbers. Practicing physicians commonly lament the sorry state of their profession. They find themselves reluctant to recommend medicine as a career for others and increasingly state that they would choose another career if they had the opportunity to "do it all over again."[1] These are significant symptoms.

The causes of this malaise in health care are many and complex. They press upon the health care professions from within and from without. In assuming a gospel perspective, I will begin this chapter with a bold claim about the causes of many of the problems medicine now faces: the practice of medicine in late twentieth century America suffers intensely from a lack of Spirit. The malaise in medicine, sensed now by so many, is at least partly, if not wholly, a spiritual malaise. Among the things medicine needs, and cannot articulate, is a genuine spirituality.

Genuine Samaritanism

When one looks to the gospel for a solution to any question about medicine, one cannot go far without coming to grips with the parable of the Good Samaritan (Lk. 10:25–37). Countless hospitals and other medical organizations claim this story as their motto or even as their name. But few are ready to accept a spirituality for medical practice based upon the demands of genuine Samaritanism.

Many are ready to donate money to help the sick, and that is certainly an appropriate lesson one can draw from the story of the Samaritan who gave money to the innkeeper for the care of a stranger left at the side of the road. Many are ready to accept the lesson that the privileged and the clergy are being urged not to shirk their responsibilities to help their fellow suffering human

39

beings, and that they stand accused by the behavior of the priest and the Levite in the story. Many are ready to accept the lesson that their neighbor is the whole of humanity, regardless of race, religion, disease, or national origin. Many even seek to follow the example of the Samaritan by choosing to enter professions where they literally do bind the wounds of the sick on a daily basis.

But while all of these interpretations are right and just and true, they are insufficient as a Christian interpretation of the parable in relation to the practice of medicine. The spirituality of healing to which Jesus calls his disciples goes much deeper. Reflecting on this parable in the thirteenth century, St. Bonaventure came closer to the core of its meaning when he wrote that "the Samaritan poured into the wounds of the half-dead wanderer the wine of fervent zeal and the oil of compassion."[2] Many clinicians do a good job of bandaging wounds. But has the profession let the wine of fervent zeal go sour? Has the oil of professional compassion dried out? If a doctor successfully resuscitates a patient, stops the hemorrhage, sets the fracture, and applies the bandages properly, but neglects the wine of zeal and the oil of compassion, that doctor has not healed in Jesus.

It should not seem strange that a book on the spiritual life should emphasize a parable about Christian action. For the Christian, contemplation and action are inherently linked. The challenge in trying to articulate a spirituality for those who claim the Good Samaritan as a model is to discover where the wine of fervent zeal and the oil of compassion come from, and how to secure and maintain these essential supplies.

Many Dwelling Places

A person's spiritual life can be defined, as I have said in chapter 1, as that person's relationship with God. To believe in God, then, is to believe that everyone has a spiritual life. Some people may neglect their life with God or ignore God altogether, just as some may neglect or ignore their parents. But if one has parents, then one has a relationship either to nurture or to neglect. And likewise, if there is a God, everyone has a relationship with God to either nurture or neglect. This is their spiritual life.

All spirituality is inherently individualized. But genuinely Christian spirituality, while *individualized*, is never *individualistic*. That is to say that, while each and every person's spiritual life retains the uniqueness and mystery given to that person by the God who has created each person, in the spiritual life God invites each person into an everlasting relationship of love. And as a relationship of love, a genuine spiritual life is never individualistic, selfish, or divorced from all the other persons in this world whose hope lies in this same loving and creative God.

Although every spiritual life is unique, there are definable clusters, patterns, and families in the spiritual life. In the Roman tradition, these have tended to be associated with the founders of religious orders—men and women whose own relationships with God have resonated deeply in the spirits of others who have subsequently chosen to follow Christ in the particular pattern of spiritual life that the saint epitomizes. Hence, there is an Augustinian spirituality, a Dominican spirituality, a Franciscan spirituality, and an Ignatian spirituality, to name just a few. As Jesus reminds us, "In my Father's house, there are many dwelling places" (Jn. 14:2).

The spirituality that I am presenting here will consequently not be an all-inclusive spirituality, for there probably is no such thing. But since I am a Franciscan Friar in the Roman Catholic Church, the spirituality presented will be a Christian spirituality, nurtured in the Roman tradition, Franciscan in character, and also necessarily quite personal. The hope of any spiritual writer must be that such work will resonate somewhere, somehow, for someone else, who is another person, in another relationship with God, possibly in another tradition. This is a hope that animates my ecumenical faith that since God is one, there is enough common ground between persons of faith that the experiences I share with readers will stimulate someone else's own love for God and for all God's people. All spirituality ultimately has the character of testimony.

Spirituality, Medicine, and the World

Spirituality cannot be a form of escapism. As Richard Niebuhr so carefully laid out, all forms of Christian spirituality and theology define themselves in relation to the culture: either against the

culture, above the culture, within the culture, in paradoxical relation to the culture, or transforming the culture.[3] Love of God and
love of neighbor are inseparable; they are two sides of the same
coin. A doctor or nurse's spiritual life cannot consist in bracketing
off the experience of the office, the clinic, the classroom, or the
laboratory in order to pray as if the office, the clinic, the classroom, or the laboratory did not exist. Doctors and nurses experience God in and through the technological medicine they
practice. If one takes the incarnation seriously, then God must be
in the midst of the medical milieu—in the patient with the somatization disorder, the CT-scan that shows recurrent carcinoma, and
the eager medical student on her first clinical rotation, at the
sharp edge of the surgeon's knife and at the tips of the internist's
palpating fingers. To deny God's presence in these moments, to
claim that God is found only in a book or a church or a piece of
bread is romantic escapism, not Christian spirituality. To appreciate this Presence is to discover the stock of oil and the cask of
wine that the Christian doctor is called to pour into the wounds of
the sick. But how can such an appreciation be possible?

Healing, Prayer, and Memory

Any health professional who reads the gospel of Luke will be
struck by the way the physician-evangelist portrays the ministry
of Jesus as largely a ministry of teaching, healing, and prayer. A
rhythm develops in the gospel of Luke, alternating between healing and prayer. After healing Simon's mother-in-law and others,
Jesus leaves the town and goes to a deserted place (Lk. 4:42).
"The report about him spread all the more, and great crowds
assembled to listen to him and to be cured of their ailments, but
he would withdraw to deserted places to pray" (Lk. 5:15–16). As
Luke presents the Great Discourse, Jesus comes down from the
mountain after praying with his disciples, and people "came to
hear him and be healed of their diseases" (Lk. 6:18). Immediately after the transfiguration, Jesus comes down from the
mountain of mystical prayer and cures a boy convulsing with
unclean spirits (Lk. 9:37–43). This is the example of Jesus, who
teaches, heals, and prays.

Health care professionals, likewise, are called to be teachers, healers, and people of prayer in imitation of the life of Jesus, the Great Physician. Jesus invites all who call themselves Christian and doctor to this rhythm of prayer and work. It is in prayer that the grapes of human experience are crushed and fermented into the wine of fervent zeal. It is in prayer that the ripe olives of praxis are squeezed to yield the abundant oil of compassion. Without prayer, one has neither. Without prayer, there will be no balm found in all of Gilead (Jer. 8:22) and doctors will merely apply dry bandages. Without prayer, no doctor or nurse will heal in the name of Jesus. Christian health care professionals have a mission. They have received a commissioning from Christ: to heal the sick and to proclaim the good news that the reign of God is at hand (Lk. 10:9).

It is not easy for physicians or other health care professionals in the late twentieth century to find time for prayer. It is not easy for oncology nurses who are calculating chemotherapy doses or for neurosurgeons who are performing delicate operations to be immediately conscious of the presence of God in any of this. Indeed, to lapse into mystic rapture with a scalpel in hand or to interrupt a patient's history in order to go to church will help no one and cannot reasonably be what Jesus expects of anyone. And Luke, the physician-evangelist, makes sure that the teaching of Jesus regarding prayer and work is not misinterpreted.

Jesus certainly wants physicians and nurses to worship and pray. But Jesus also interrupts the Sabbath rest to cure a woman, stooped over and weakened by an unclean spirit (Lk. 13:10–17), and on another Sabbath he cures a man from dropsy (Lk. 14:1–6), over the objections of the Pharisees. Luke must have known from his own experience that patients in need of healing present on God's schedule and not the schedule of human beings. Indeed, the hours when doctors receive calls from patients can, at times, appear quite inhuman! But in Luke's account of the teaching of Jesus, he chose to remember the Sabbath cures of Jesus, perhaps to remind physicians in particular that the act of healing is itself a portal to the sacred, a participation in the mysteries of the Creator, an act of worship worthy of the Sabbath. So no physician or nurse ought to feel guilty for missing church on Sunday or being unable to make a particular Bible study session because of commitments to patient care.

But balance is essential. It is a mistake to allow oneself to become so busy that one has no time for prayer. No matter how good the work, no matter how great the needs, God does not want any one of his children to work unto physical and spiritual death. The needs of the sick are literally infinite. Absolute healing can mean nothing short of eternal life, and no human being can give that sort of healing. When Jesus said "The poor you always have with you, but me you will not always have" (Jn. 12:8), perhaps he was warning of this danger to the spiritual life. Jesus may be saying, "Your patients you will always have with you." The needs of patients will always be greater than any physician or nurse can address. Like Sisyphus, physicians and nurses can condemn themselves to an impossible task if they think that they are indispensable and that they must cure all their patients' ills. After all, the cemeteries are full of indispensable physicians and nurses. It is God, not the health care professional, who is indispensable. In thinking otherwise, the practice of medicine will quickly become dry and narrow, lifeless and dispirited. Physicians and nurses have a profound need to take time for prayer. Without such time, they may actually find themseves doing less than they feel called to do for their patients.

This, then, is the rhythm in which the spiritual life of physicians and nurses is composed. The work of healing is an experience of God's own life and love, worthy of the Sabbath. But the work of healing will be diminished if it is allowed to fill up the day so completely that it crowds out any possibility that time might be set aside for both the private and the public moments of prayer. To neglect prayer is to undermine the basis by which an appreciation of the sanctity of healing is maintained: to reduce the work of practice to the application of dry bandages. Within this basic rhythm of practice and prayer, there are as many possible spiritualities as there are symphonies. And each physician or nurse is called to write the symphony for which God has commissioned him or her.

Physicians and nurses can ask the Spirit for the gift of wisdom. Orchestrating prayer, family, and work is not easy. But it is essential to realize that the proper balance can *only* be discovered in prayer. God has a precise composition in mind for everyone. And God has given everyone the necessary tools to accomplish this orchestration—silence, memory, and imagination.

"Had not the Lord been with us, let Israel say," writes the psalmist (Ps. 124:1). The grammatical construction employed here, a recurrent one throughout the Psalms, is instructive. In English, this construction would be called a contrary-to-fact past perfect conditional. What the Psalms invite us to, over and over, is a stance in prayer in which the past is perfected, in which the past is gratefully remembered, and in which God is praised. It is of course not possible, except in rare instances, to break through an actual clinical event into an explicit and conscious moment of prayer. One can be grateful for such moments when they come and accept them as gifts from God. But far more often it is only at the end of a long and busy day—when the office is finally empty; when the rounding is done and all the calls have stopped; when dinner has grown cold and waits, wrapped in lonely plastic in the microwave at home; when one's loving spouse and children are already fast asleep—that one begins to wonder whether the life of the physician is really worth it after all. It is only then that one might, taking the scriptures from the shelf, read in Psalm 71:9, "Cast me not off in my old age; as my strength fails, forsake me not," and experience the sudden grace of a moment of prayer in which it all comes, briefly, into focus, as one remembers from the 9:30 A.M. appointment, the 95-year-old woman with Alzheimer's disease and her daughter with all their struggles—the daughter's fierce tears and deep love and the vacant suffering eyes of the woman whose mind can no longer understand anything of the murmuring sounds one has heard in the sunken hollow of her chest. And finally, finally, one understands briefly what it means to heal, because one remembers what it felt like to be a healing presence, and one remembers that truly, God was there. "Had not the Lord been at my side." This is the physician's song.

The clinical moment remembered in the silence of prayer is a sweet grape pressed into a fervent zeal for practice. The patient remembered in prayer is a ripe olive from which the golden oil of compassion is wrought.

The Patient as Textbook

William Osler once wrote that "it is a safe rule to have no teaching without a patient for a text, and the best teaching is that taught by the patient himself."[4] Patients can, of course, teach physicians and nurses spiritual as well as medical lessons, and it is critical for a Christian physician or nurse to appreciate this. Such a stance requires the utmost humility of the clinician and a profound sense of respect for the patient.

Some may believe that the Christian physician or nurse is bringing the healing presence of Christ to the patient, that the physician or nurse is a conduit for grace, an instrument of the healing power of God. There is much to be said for such an approach to the spirituality of medical practice. It cannot be said that such an approach is wrong. But different approaches may also help to stimulate growth in the spiritual life. I would like to suggest another approach, in the hope that it might excite the reader's prayerful imagination in ways that might bring him or her even closer to the mystery of Christian healing.

When St. Francis of Assisi was a young man, after he had decided that he did not wish to be a cloth merchant like his father, after his dream of knighthood had been crushed by a prolonged illness, after a series of unusual dreams that he thought had great significance but could not fully understand, but before he had discerned his ultimate vocation in life, it is said that he was walking along a road on the outskirts of Assisi with his friend Leo, when he thought he heard a bell. It was not the bright sound of a church bell, but a coarse, flat, pedestrian clank something like a cowbell, yet with a darker timbre. Francis was frightened by the sound. It was unpleasant, yet familiar. It began to come closer. His friend Leo became frightened as they suddenly both realized what the bell meant. "Let's get out of here, Francis," Leo cried. But Francis, not knowing exactly why, stood his ground. Leo pleaded again, but Francis, now trembling, would not run. Suddenly, over the hill just ahead, there appeared a deformed figure with a clanging bell around the neck. Francis's heart pounded. His nostrils burned with the pungent smell of rotting flesh. The figure waved him off, but Francis did not move. "A leper," he thought to himself. "I have always been repulsed by the sight of lepers! How much I have feared their dread contagion!"

"Have you not heard my bell?" asked the leper. "Do you not know that I am forced to wear this bell to warn you that a leper is approaching?"

Francis remained motionless, tasting his fear as he swallowed. Then suddenly, filled with a strength which came he knew not from where, Francis ran toward the leper, now much more frightened than he. Francis embraced the leper, kissed him on his festering cheek, and wept aloud, "Brother leper, forgive me for neglecting you." Then, for a moment, the leper's appearance was transformed. For a moment, he seemed to wear a crown of thorns and to bleed from wounds in his hands, his feet, and his sides. He looked at Francis with love. And then, just as suddenly, the leper vanished from sight, leaving Francis weeping on the silent road. Francis turned to his friend Leo, who had been watching dumfounded from a distance.

"Brother Leo, don't you see? Don't you see? The lepers," he said, "they all turn into Christ!" Francis had found his vocation.[5]

Now, most physicians and nurses will not have such dramatic experiences. Nonetheless, the essential point of the story is that physicians and nurses and other health care professionals can find an experience of Christ in practice, not so much as the One who guides their hands or the One who practices at their side, but rather by seeing Christ in the patients they serve. Christ may call at 3 A.M. to report acute abdominal pain. Christ may roll into the emergency room in shock, suffering from a gunshot wound to the chest. Christ may be thirteen years old, unwed, pregnant, and in labor. Christ may be ninety years old and slowly dying of congestive heart failure. This is a way of seeing the practice of medicine that can become a rich spiritual harvest. This is a way to gather the grapes and the olives that can be processed by prayerful remembrance into the balm of true healing, eradicating cynicism, arrogance, complacency, and despair. This is a way to be open to the presence of God's healing power and grace. Christ certainly *does* look over the shoulder of the clinician in one sense; but in another, perhaps deeper sense, Christ looks, through suffering eyes, directly at the clinician. He says, "Whatever you did for one of these least brothers of mine, you did for me" (Mt. 25:40).

If they are open to the experience, physicians and nurses will be amazed at the intimacy with which Christ makes himself known to them. He invites those who doubt to put their hands into his wounds (Jn. 20:24–30); to put their hands through the blade's incision and feel the blood, the water, and the guts; and to dispel all gnostic doubts that God would ever share in the human condition (1 Jn. 5:6). God becomes vulnerable for the sake of all people (cf. Heb. 2:5–18), and God's weakness is more powerful than the chair of any department in any medical school (cf. 1 Cor. 1:25). This vulnerability means that much will be demanded of the physician to whom the life of the patient is entrusted. But the physician who understands the vulnerability of the patient to be the vulnerability of God will be precisely the kind of physician who *can* be trusted.

The Wounded Healer

The poet T.S. Eliot can help illuminate yet another way of seeing the spiritual meaning in the clinician-patient relationship. Writing of Christ, Eliot uses the metaphor of the physician in a manner that physicians, nurses, and other health care professionals might prayerfully consider:

> The wounded surgeon plies the steel
> That questions the distempered part;
> Beneath the bleeding hands we feel
> The sharp compassion of the healer's art
> Resolving the enigma of the fever chart.[6]

All health care professionals are wounded healers. They cannot escape suffering themselves. Moments of pain, loneliness, fatigue, and sacrifice are intrinsic to the human condition. The physician or nurse's own bleeding can become the source of the compassion in the healer's art. From the physician's or nurse's own suffering can come the wine of fervent zeal and the oil of compassion. As St. Bonaventure writes, "The strong and the healthy do not suffer as a sick person does and hence may have no compassion with the sick. But they will know it later on when they themselves suffer affliction."[7] It may not be now that the physician or nurse suffers; but past or present or future, every clinician has experiences of suffering. The physician's or nurse's wounds can become resources for healing in the mystical paradox of Christian living and dying.

In the silence of prayer, the health care professional's own pain will surface. In silence before God, there is no place to hide. The clinician's brokenness can no longer be covered up by a frenetic work schedule or delusions of invincibility. In the silence of prayer, clinicians can come to know the truth about themselves, a truth that will set them free (cf. Jn. 8:32). A clinician's own loneliness can remind him or her that no other person can love a patient, a physician, a nurse, or physician's assistant, or anyone else with the overwhelming and absolutely unconditional love with which God loves all people. The clinician's own sense of mortality can be a sign of the absolute and unconditional dependence of all living creatures—patients, physicians, nurses, physician's assistants, and pneumococci—on the creating and sustaining power of God Almighty. The clinician's own sense of pain can be a reminder of the pain Jesus suffered and a sign that the pain of the physician and the pain of the patient can be unified and redeemed by the pain of Christ. The bandages such a clinician applies will not be dry. A clinician who appreciates these mysteries will necessarily be fervent in zeal for practice and compassionate toward all patients.

As the late Henri Nouwen is careful to remind us, it would be unwise to allow the care rendered by a wounded healer to degenerate into cheap exhibitionism.[8] This is true for ministers and, perhaps, even truer for physicians and nurses. The parishioner does not come to the pastor to hear about the pastor's problems. The patient does not come to the physician to hear about the physician's problems. Rather, the oil of compassion consists of a silent sense of understanding, of caring, of attention, of time well spent that communicates far more than words can tell. The care delivered by a healer aware of the healer's own woundedness softens the tone of Oslerian *Aequanimitas,*[9] yet does not completely eradicate the notion. Wounded healers, as we will discuss in chapter 7, cannot become so overwhelmed with emotional reaction to the pain of others that they are unable to render effective care. Competence remains the first act of compassion. Wounded healers do not ask their patients for help, but recognize the unity between their own neediness and the needs of their patients. Wounded healers issue an invitation to patients to enter into the space of the healing relationship. In this sense, the clinician offers hospitality.

Hospital and hospitality are related words, sharing a common etymology in the Latin *hospitalis,* 'relating to a guest.' To be hospitable to patients is not to treat them only as a series of problems to be solved. To be hospitable to patients is to eschew the attitude of "getting rid of patients" that often begins with internship and may pervade the duration of a physician's career.[10] To be hospitable is to make one's guests feel important, worthy of one's time and effort. Hospitals and those who work there are called to strive to make their patients feel important. Henri Nouwen has articulated three concrete signs that characterize the healing of those aware of their own woundedness. These are the signs of hospitality: concentration, compassion, and perspective.[11]

Concentration means paying attention to the needs of one's guests or patients. It means recognizing their importance as persons and the importance of their projects and concerns. It means attention to detail. In medicine, this does not mean merely noticing that the albumin concentration is beginning to drop, but also noticing when the patient's spirits begin to drop. It means anticipating and preventing not only postoperative pulmonary emboli, but also the fears a patient may have about dying during surgery, and taking the time necessary to understand how this might be caused by memories of a parent who died under anaesthesia twenty years before.

Compassion means, at the very least, "feeling with" the patient. But it is not just what the physician or nurse feels regarding the plight of the patient. It is not a simple awareness of countertransferences. For the Christian, compassion means a radical understanding of the essential unity between one's own suffering and the suffering of another, a unity grounded in the suffering of Jesus. To suffer is bad enough. To suffer alone is a far worse fate.

The Christian clinician has the opportunity to communicate to the patient, even if more often implicitly than explicitly, an understanding of the bond that unites the suffering of all persons and redeems that suffering from abject lonely despair. Christian compassion brings to the patient's bedside an awareness of the possibility of redemption from the meaninglessness of suffering, because the Christian physician or nurse is aware of the suffering, death, and resurrection of Jesus Christ. A quiet smile and a gentle touch, if done in Jesus, may be all that is required to communicate the gifts of faith, hope, and love. This can be a soothing balm for the wounded, poured out by a Samaritan who can be a Good Samaritan only because he knows that he also suffers, and that his and all other human suffering is redeemed in Jesus Christ.

The *perspective* required is to see the wounds of patients as true signs of God and as portals of hope. How often has illness marked the turning point in the conversion stories of the saints! Saul did not find God until he was knocked off a horse and blinded (Acts 9:1–19). The conversion of Francis of Assisi began while he was sick and imprisoned.[12] Ignatius of Loyola was recovering from gunshot wounds when he first began to read and take the words of sacred scripture seriously.[13] Physicians and nurses are privileged with the opportunity to see how God speaks to God's own people in and through their illnesses.

The Christian physician or nurse will bring to the bedside the perspective that sees the presence of God in the wounds of patients and hope in the midst of illness. The Christian physician or nurse lets the patient know, often through very subtle gestures and words, that this is a perspective to which the patient is invited and a perspective the patient is welcome to share with the physician or nurse. The Christian physician or nurse is, in this sense, hospitable to the patient, giving time and space to the patient so that this perspective might be nurtured. A physician or nurse who fears death, finds suffering meaningless, and is desperately trying to fill life's voids with superficial pleasures and material goods will never give the patient permission to express true hope and faith in the midst of illness. Neither will such a physician or nurse ever recognize and therefore share that perspective with a patient who has already found it. Such a physician or nurse will merely apply dry bandages and leave the room, but will never truly heal.

When patients respond with faith in the midst of profound physical calamity, a physician or nurse who has the right perspective can find his or her own faith strengthened by the experiences of the patients. When dying patients respond with true hope, not a naive hope for cure that is really only psychological denial disguised as hope, but with genuine Christian hope rooted in the resurrection, a clinician with the right perspective will be able to recognize that hope and feel that virtue nurtured in his or her own life. When illness clarifies for patients and their families the central importance of love, a clinician with the right perspective will learn more about the power of love, which is the very life of God. And when patients collapse spiritually in the face of illness, a clinician with the right perspective will understand much more acutely how desperate their plight really is and will treat the wounds of such patients with even more liberal applications of the wine of fervent zeal and of the oil of compassion.

Conclusion

Christian health care professionals are called to cultivate a spirituality of medical practice. The spiritual dimensions of the practice of the healing arts are clearly integral to the work of doctors and nurses. Christian physicians and nurses are called to develop a rhythm of work and prayer in imitation of the ministry of Jesus, allowing work and prayer to enrich each other. Prayer informs the life of practice, and practice informs the life of prayer. To neglect either is to become unbalanced. Christian physicians and nurses can bring to health care what seems sorely lacking in contemporary practice—the wine of fervent zeal and the oil of compassion.

Christian health care professionals can learn to recognize the face of Christ in the faces of their patients and to recognize in their own suffering the bond that especially links clinicians with their patients: the redemptive suffering of Jesus Christ. For it is true, as scripture tells us, that "by his stripes we were healed" (Is. 53:5; 1 Pt. 2:24).

In the midst of the pressures and the hurry and the intense concentration that technological medicine makes necessary, it is important for Christian physicians and nurses to take time for prayerful reflection on the awesome mysteries that open out before them on a daily basis. To neglect prayer is to "tread out the olive, yet pour no oil, and the grapes, yet drink no wine" (Mi. 6:15). Memory becomes integral to prayer. Clinical experiences can be integrated with the reading of scripture, the singing of hymns, and the quiet of intimate moments with God.

Physicians and nurses are called to allow the Holy Spirit to guide their imaginations as they pray and read scripture. This is obviously what St. Bonaventure did. On might surmise that he asked himself, "What point might God be making for me, at this moment in my life, when the parable states that the Samaritan dressed the stranger's wounds with wine and oil?"

Christian health care professionals are also people of genuine hospitality, who welcome patients into the space of Christian healing and invite them to share their stories of faith, hope, and love. The clinician's jar will thus be replenished with the oil of compassion the more he or she pours into the wounds of the sick. And the jug of this oil will not run dry, as God has foretold through Elijah (1 Kgs. 17:16).

The Christian clinician prays for patients, prays with patients, and prays the prayers of patients. The Christian clinician will pray in the car, pray in the church, pray before bed, pray in the library, pray between patients in the office—wherever and whenever it is possible. The total time spent is not so important as the intention. For what God requires is enough prayer "only to do the right and to love goodness, and to walk humbly with your God" (Mi. 6:8). This is the spirit in which health care professionals can become healers, and strangers can become Good Samaritans.

Chapter 4

God-Talk at the Bedside

Believe it or not, data are now accumulating about the effect of religious beliefs on health outcomes. One of my colleagues at Georgetown, Dr. Dale Matthews, has even prepared an annotated bibliography of this literature.[1] The studies are variable in quality, but some are actually quite well done. I'll cite a few facts that seem well established and come from high quality, peer-reviewed medical journals.

1. Americans, in general, are a religious people; 95 percent believe in God, and 57 percent report praying at least once a day.
2. Physicians, on the other hand, are substantially less religious than the rest of the population at large. This is especially true of psychiatrists. Only 43 percent of psychiatrists say they believe in God.
3. In a study of 1,014 male physicians graduating from the Johns Hopkins Medical School between 1948 and 1964, lack of religious affiliation was the strongest predictor for subsequent development of alcoholism. Physicians who developed alcoholism were greater than four times more likely to declare that they had no religious affiliation compared with physicians who did not become alcoholics.
4. Religious affiliation is positively correlated with the psychological well-being of patients. In a study of 272 elderly outpatients, religious activity was significantly and positively correlated with happiness, sense of usefulness, and personal adjustment.
5. The classical study on church attendance and health was conducted by Dr. Comstock of the Johns Hopkins School of Hygiene and Public Health, involving 100,000 people in Washington County, Maryland in the 1970s. The study found that those who attended church once a week or more had 50 percent fewer deaths from coronary artery disease, emphysema, and suicide and 75 percent fewer deaths from cirrhosis.

6. Mormons and Seventh Day Adventists appear to have better survival rates than the general population.
7. At least one study, from Alameda County, California, showed the effects of church membership on mortality rates to be independent of smoking, drinking, obesity, activity, and socioeconomic status.

In all, Dr. Matthews reviewed 212 peer-reviewed studies of religious commitment and health. He found that 75 percent showed a positive impact, 17 percent showed a mixed or neutral impact, and 7 percent showed a negative impact. The take-home message would appear to be that religion is good for your health. But there are two very interesting nuances to this conclusion:

1. These findings regarding better health outcomes are associated with some measure of actual religious *commitment,* such as self-reported strength of belief or reports of actual religious practices (*e.g.,* spiritual reading or church or temple attendance), not just reporting the denomination in which one was raised.
2. These effects appear to be independent of denomination. Regardless of the actual faith one professes, practicing that faith, or expressing a strong commitment to that faith, provides the relevant independent variable that predicts better health outcomes. One might call this epidemiological ecumenism!

Despite this data, I think it is fair to say that America has witnessed an enormous decline in the extent to which physicians and other health care professionals concern themselves with the religious beliefs of their patients. Religion appears to be important to most Americans (and therefore to most American patients), and religious commitment appears to be correlated with good health outcomes. But when was the last time anyone heard an American doctor or nurse or physician's assistant ask about the patient's religious and spiritual concerns? When was the last time anyone involved in health care saw a patient's chart in which any health care professional noted the patient's religious beliefs?

Several years ago, I performed a chart review study, looking at the quality of care rendered to patients with "Do Not Resuscitate" orders. In the 103 charts my colleagues and I examined, not one contained any note from any health care professional regarding the religious beliefs of the patient or any religious concerns the patient might have or any attempt to see whether or not the patient wanted to talk to someone from the pastoral care department or with personal clergy.[2] Despite the fact that the decision to have a "Do Not Resuscitate" order might be the most momentous decision any patient ever faces, a decision of enormous personal and potentially transcendent significance, and in spite of the fact that patients, by and large, think about themselves and these issues in religious terms, health care professionals did not think these concerns important enough to address.

Why the Taboo?

Why don't we health care professionals talk to our patients about religion? Is it because we think the subject is too private? I can't speak for other health care professionals, but the HIV epidemic now has me asking regularly about sexual practices in rather graphic detail—how many partners, what sorts of sexual acts, with what protective devices? That seems pretty private, but because it has an impact on health, it's OK to ask.

Is it because health care professionals believe that the patient's religious beliefs are irrelevant? Perhaps if one were only to look at studies that have asked the rather insensitive question of religious denomination, one could come to such a conclusion. But if the data I presented are to be believed, then the patient's degree of religious commitment is hardly irrelevant to medicine, even if it should turn out that none of these results are statistically independent of social supports, diet, sexual practices, stress, alcohol and drug consumption, cigarette use, and so forth. And even if these intriguing data are eventually borne out by subsequent study, the fact that religion is important to patients seems to be justification enough. Asking whether the patient affiliates himself or herself with any particular religion and how strongly he or she identifies with that religion or to what extent he or she practices it is hardly the same as asking to which political party he or she belongs. Unless the answer to the latter is that the patient belongs to a white supremacist group, political affiliation is hardly relevant to health.

Is it because health care professionals are embarrassed? Well, I think that as professionals, we'll just need to get over that.

But if it is because a health care professional is unsure or frankly dismissive of religion personally, there is a grave problem. A professional can't allow his or her own beliefs to so dominate the practitioner-patient relationship that what's important for the patient is never allowed to surface.

It does seem, indeed, as if religion is the last taboo in medicine. But I think that health care professionals can be persuaded of the need to overcome this taboo, and for two reasons. The first is the relationship between religious belief and health that I described above. But even if it were the case that religious belief had *no* impact on health, there is a second, and perhaps more important, reason. It is because if health care professionals are to value their patients as *persons,* then they have an obligation to be respectful of what is of importance to them. To ignore the religious beliefs of a religious patient is to ignore the patient.

If God is God, then God is the most important thing there is. And when a religious person becomes ill, what is important to him or to her becomes clearer. I do not know to what extent other health care professionals share my experience, but there are times when I feel that I need to take off my shoes before entering the room of a critically ill patient who is facing that illness in faith, in hope, and in love. For me, these moments are genuine experiences of the sacred, because what really matters has become clearer to the patient. The triviality that so dominates our culture is revealed for what it is in the face of the awesome mysteries of life, death, and God. Such an experience can be a moment of epiphany for physicians, nurses, and other health care professionals who are sometimes lulled into thinking that what matters is that the patient be discharged before the HMO says the allotted hospital days are up.

So in some ways, it does not matter to me that religious belief has any connection whatsoever to health outcomes. The health outcomes are a bonus. What matters is that religion matters to the patient. And if I am to respect that patient as a person, then I have a duty to be respectful of what matters to him or to her. And if religion is the patient's ultimate value, this implies respect for the patient's religious beliefs. But I cannot be respectful of the patient's religious beliefs if I am unaware that the patient has any such beliefs.

Talking with Patients About God

In a very pluralistic society like our own, big questions arise about how and when to engage the question of God with patients. It is perhaps helpful in this regard to look at how the beliefs of the health care professional and the patient match up, and how this context might affect the ways in which religious questions are engaged in the clinician-patient relationship. A simple (and admittedly, somewhat simplistic) way of doing this would be to look at four possibilities:

1. When the health care professional believes in God and the patient believes in God (which statistics suggest is a common state of affairs), then the big question is not a problem at all. Both will be able to talk about religion in relationship to healing. The theoretical problems in such cases are only over differences in denomination and in strength of belief.

2. When neither the health care professional nor the patient believes in God, then things might appear to be at their simplest. If neither party is interested in things spiritual, the question will simply be irrelevant to both parties. On the other hand, if the parties do not consider the question irrelevant despite their lack of belief, or if they consider themselves "spiritual" despite their lack of theism, things may be at their most complex. Without any sense of common language or organizing principle for beliefs, or even rudimentary understanding of the beliefs of the other as an identifiable and organized religion with an accompanying spirituality, it will be extraordinarily difficult to engage in anything other than an acknowledgment of the existence of a private system of transcendent belief. The parties to such a conversation

will lack the common assumptions and common vocabulary with which to engage each other in the questions. For those who believe that spirituality is always "spirituality-for-me," others will always have limited access to that spirituality. Sadly, beyond a polite acknowledgment that spiritual concerns are important, those who reject the notion of God but still accept some sense of transcendence will find that they will have to struggle mightily to find a way to say anything to each other about things spiritual. The problem of private spiritualities is linked to the problem of private languages.

3. When the patient believes in God and the health care professional does not, (and statistics predict that this will be the most common situation) then I think that what I have already discussed about respect for the patient and about the association between religious commitment and health outcomes would suggest that the physician might take the initiative to make inquiries about the patient's religious beliefs and to be supportive and perhaps even encouraging of that patient's beliefs. Even an atheist who rejects the very possibility of transcendent or spiritual meaning can know something, even anthropological, about various religions and their belief systems and vocabulary and can engage patients in discussions about these beliefs that can prove fruitful for the patient.

4. When the health care professional believes in God and the patient does not (a situation that statistics predict is the least common of the four scenarios), one might encounter some controversy. This controversy can arise because of the health care professional's interpretation of the meaning of the data suggesting that religion is good for one's health. The believing clinician then has two reasons to want to bring up religion. One is the desire, as a believer, to spread the faith. The other is a desire, as a clinician, to encourage the patient to engage in practices that are good for the patient's health. Both are in themselves good goals. But one needs to be very cautious about interpreting what these goals imply.

Why Data on Health Outcomes of Belief
Do Not Justify Proselytizing

Earlier, I suggested a second justification for raising the question of religion in the setting of the clinician-patient relationship—that respect for the patient is an ethical imperative and that respect for the patient demands respect for what the patient considers to be of ultimate importance. I will argue, however, that this same premise, while justifying the introduction of the religious question in the clinician-patient relationship, also precludes the all-too-easy conclusion that the believing clinician should actively encourage religious belief for patients who do not profess a religious belief system.

Edmund Pellegrino and David Thomasma observe that when the physician swears an oath to serve the good of the patient, the good of the patient can be read in an expansive manner. They describe a four-fold notion of the patient's good.[3] The first level of the patient's good is the biomedical good; the second level is the good of the patient's particular choices of the good; the third level is the good of the patient as a person, endowed with an indelible dignity; and the fourth level is the ultimate good as the patient sees it.

For a religious patient, the ultimate good will be God. For unbelieving patients, this might be the net social welfare, a humanistic view of human virtue, or the good of the ecosystem. The important point is that these four levels of the patient's good are arranged hierarchically. The biomedical good of the patient occupies the lowest rung on this ladder of the good. Medicine serves the good of the patient as a whole person in and through the biomedical good, but the biomedical good of the patient is not the sole or even the primary concern of the physician. The physician addresses concerns regarding the biomedical good of the patient in the context of considering the good of the patient as a whole person. Thus, for example, it is generally morally appropriate not to dialyze a competent patient whose particular choice is not to be dialyzed, because one is obliged to respect that patient as a free and dignified person who may be making that decision, in the context of belief, that eternal happiness with God is waiting on the other side of renal failure after a long life of suffering. Even though dialysis would serve the biomedical good of this patient, it would not serve the good of this patient as a whole person.

And so it is with the case of the believing clinician and the unbelieving patient. Even if it is the case that religious commitment would improve the health of unbelieving patients in a biomedical sense, this is not a warrant to persuade patients to commit themselves to religion. The biomedical good of the patient is the lowest level on the hierarchy of the patient's good. If the patient's sense of the ultimate good does not include God, it is important that the patient's unbelief be respected if the patient is to be respected as a whole person and if the doctor is to serve the good of the patient as a whole person. Just as one must respect the wish of a Jehovah's Witness not to be transfused even though this might result in a poor health outcome, so one must respect the lack of religious beliefs of an unbelieving patient, even if it is the case that this will mean a poorer health outcome for that patient. After all, it takes a lot of faith to be an atheist. A good doctor will respect such faith, even if the doctor disagrees.

There is a second argument against allowing clinicians to actively encourage religious belief and practice among their patients. This can be called an "internal" argument. Those "inside" faith communities might seriously question whether or not it is theologically appropriate to encourage religious belief on the basis of the fact that it will improve a person's health outcomes. I cannot speak with authority regarding other religions, but from the perspective of Catholic Christianity, this would represent a seriously distorted theology. If faith means, first and foremost, a love relationship with a personal God, then it seems obvious that it would be an unhealthy relationship if it were based on its benefits for the lover. Husbands and wives who truly love each other do not do so because of what they each can "get" out of the relationship. The first concern of true love is giving. To say, "I love God because it will help me to live a longer and healthier life," contradicts the meaning of love. To encourage another person to fall in love with God because it will yield health benefits is a fundamental distortion of what the love of God means. While love of God can have, as the figures above show, demonstrable positive effects upon health, it is also true that love of God can be very, very bad for one's health. Christians need look no further than to the example of the saints, the martyrs, and the crucifixion of Jesus Christ.

Finally, one needs to acknowledge that the relationship between a health care professional and a patient is not a relationship among equals. As human persons, made in the image and likeness of God, both are certainly equal. But in terms of knowledge and power, the professional always has the upper hand. Because of this imbalance in knowledge and power, there is great potential for the professional to take advantage of the vulnerability of the patient. It is critically important that health care professionals, out of respect for patients, be trusted not to take advantage of this imbalance in freedom, vulnerability, knowledge, and power. It is for these reasons that physicians have long held that it is never proper to engage in sexual relationships with their patients. For similar reasons, the proselytizing of patients would seem universally improper.

How Might One Talk With Patients About God?

Practical questions arise about how and when health care professionals might ascertain the religious beliefs of their patients and precisely what kinds of conversations and practices might be encouraged. As far as I know, there are no data about these issues, so much of what I will say will consist of anecdotes and reflections. I hope these will prove useful and will provide an opportunity for readers to reflect on their own practices and experiences.

Routine Questions

I have begun to include questions about religion in the social history as part of my routine new patient history. Just as inquiries about quantity of alcohol consumed are not useful, so merely asking denomination, if the data I presented earlier are to be believed, is not useful. I have begun to ask the fairly open-ended and, I think, nonjudgmental question: "What role does religion play in your life?" I should point out that some patients come to me specifically because they know that I am a Franciscan Friar. I also suspect that some avoid me specifically because I am a Franciscan Friar. But by and large, most people don't have the foggiest notion of what "O.F.M." stands for and come to see me for the same reasons that they go to see any other internist.

I've used this question routinely now for about two years. I have a very limited academic physician's practice, so that doesn't amount to a huge number, perhaps 60 new patients. Only one patient has raised questions about the question, asking, with a bit of a sharp edge to her tone, whether this was something Georgetown did because it was a Catholic hospital. She seemed satisfied by my explanation that I had asked her, as I had asked all my patients, because studies have shown that religion is important to most patients.

Most patients have told me a good deal about the extent of their religious commitment. In keeping with the statistics, most have expressed belief in God and some form of religious practice. Almost all have seemed pleased that I have asked.

Clues

Sometimes patients, particularly inpatients, surround themselves with religious symbols and the like. I no longer ignore the open Bible or the Koran or the rosary beads or the Shabbat candles at the bedside. I ask, "I'm sorry if I disturbed you. Were you praying? Would you prefer that I come back a little later?" I often then tell them that I'll pray for them too, or put my comments into a religious context, or say, "Let's pray that you don't need the operation. But if it should become necessary to operate, let's pray that God will be with you and the surgeon."

I have also found that patients often drop more subtle hints about their religious beliefs and their desire to talk about it. This is especially true in the outpatient setting.

I don't think clinicians can afford to ignore these hints any more than clinicians can afford to ignore other hints patients give when they try to test out whether or not it is safe to talk about personal matters. If the patient mutters, "Well, I guess it's in God's hands," or some other such phrase, clinicians cannot ignore it. I try to respond to such comments by asking, "Do you think God will take care of it?" or, in a more indirect fashion, "Well, God does have big hands." Such comments are often followed by patient responses, "Indeed God does. I pray to God for help every day. My whole church prays for me too." And we're off and running.

Dropping Hints

In a more daring fashion, I often drop hints that I'm a believing person with whom the patient can feel free to talk about their health concerns in a religious context. I often end patient sessions by simply saying, "God bless." Sometimes patients pick up on this and if so, I often go a bit further and tell them that I'll pray for them.

And I do pray for my patients. Almost on a daily basis I pray for one or another of my patients, particularly those who seem most troubled in spirit—especially those with the painful mixture of physical and psychiatric disease or those with substance abuse.

Praying with Patients

On rare occasions, I have prayed with patients. I do not, however, pray with patients on a one to one basis at the bedside or in the exam room, at least not in the capacity of the attending physician. I leave that sort of praying to the chaplains. Perhaps this is cowardice on my part, but I think not. I think that the roles of the pastoral care team and the medical team are distinct, even if interrelated and mutually enhancing. When I am a patient's doctor, I am *not* that patient's pastor. There are some things that a patient might want to tell clergy that he or she would not want to tell the doctor, and there are some things that a patient might want to tell a doctor that he or she would not want to tell a pastor or rabbi.

This brings up a point for me, as a Franciscan Friar. I am a brother, not a priest. Some people have asked me whether or not I wouldn't find it wonderful to be able to anoint my patients, for example. I think not. I honestly think that patients could get confused. I think that they need both medical care and pastoral care, and even though I am among the first to say that ideally these two teams will work closely together for the good of the patient, I am also among the first to say that it is preferable that the boundaries between these two professions be maintained.

So, I have been present for the administration of the sacrament of the sick to some of my patients. I have prayed the Our Father with families gathered around the bed of a dying patient. It has seemed good, natural, wholesome, and correct. It has never been forced.

At the right time and in the right place it has been the right thing. But I have been there as a co-participant in the patient's religious expression. I have not presided over that religious expression.

Funerals

A final area of interest is whether to go to the funeral of a patient. I have done so three times. Once I attended the funeral of a homeless schizophrenic woman who had been referred to me by a group of priests and nuns who had met her in the course of their urban ministry and had noted her deteriorating medical condition. She had no known family. Her funeral service was arranged by and attended by the religiously motivated clergy and lay people who worked at a shelter and support services center for the homeless. I attended at their invitation.

On another occasion I attended the funeral of a severely mentally retarded middle-aged man whose sister had cared for him ever since their parents had died. He was a wonderful man who was mute, but used to communicate his thanks by kissing my hand at the end of each office visit. He developed significant heart and kidney disease in his late 40s. At age 50, he had an angioplasty (I had to convince the cardiologists that he was both able to cooperate and worthy of their services). But when his kidneys began to shut down for good at age 52, his sister and I decided that he just wouldn't be able to handle dialysis without being heavily sedated for every session and that such a procedure would be an extraordinary burden for him. He died slowly and peacefully. Attending his funeral seemed absolutely the natural thing to do. Attending helped me to attain closure.

Wilda's Story

The most memorable funeral I attended was for a woman with whom I had shared very frank religious conversations over the course of her terminal illness. Wilda was Episcopalian. I learned from her family the day after her death that she had specifically requested that I read the prayers of petition during her funeral.

Wilda had severe coronary artery disease. She had discovered that I was a Franciscan Friar shortly after her left main coronary artery bypass operation. Several days after the operation, which was highly risky and at least initially successful, she told me that she had known that it would be OK. The night before the operation, she said, she had a dream that a man in a long brown robe and a hood had stood at the foot of her bed and whispered to her that it would be OK. And she knew it would.

Like many things in the spiritual life, this could have been a coincidence. However, if one believes that God is never absent from human experience, one's interpretation of the miraculous depends more on the way in which God's presence is made manifest than it does God's presence or absence. I do not believe that God was any more or less present to this patient than to any other patient. But my interpretation of her experience and her interpretation of her own experience and her willingness to share that experience with me constituted the miraculous in that event. In any case, I was, of course, flabbergasted and had to share with her the fact that I was a friar. "It was St. Francis," she replied. "I knew it. I just knew it."

From that moment on, there was a special bond between us. When her graft clotted and she was declared inoperable and began to experience a long series of small heart attacks, I was privileged to watch a woman of enormous faith and goodness face her death with the fullness of human dignity. We talked often about God, family, life, and death. She had not asked for suffering. She had not asked to become so dependent upon her family. But she did not flee from suffering when faced with the choice either to love or to avoid love and the suffering love entails. She did not flee from suffering when faced with the choice either to embrace life or to annihilate life and the suffering life entails.

Her family rallied around her. When we decided that hospitalization no longer served any purpose, we decided together to treat her subsequent presumed myocardial infarcts with nitroglycerin and morphine at home. Her daughter and the hospice nurse probably treated three more small heart attacks at home in the last three months until her long Lent was over. She died on Easter Sunday morning.

If I had not been asked, I guess I probably would not have attended her funeral. But that would have been a mistake. I needed to be there. And in her own way, I guess she knew that. I needed to be there to mourn the loss, not just of a patient, but of a spiritual friend—a holy woman who inspires me to this very day.

May God Show You

St. Francis once wrote, "I have done what was mine to do. May God show you what is yours."[4]

I don't really know whose funerals to attend or with whom to pray. I have no secret formula to offer other health care professionals. Perhaps I have attended too few funerals and prayed with too few patients. I know also that I have neither the time nor the stamina to attend the funerals of all my patients who die. But I do know that on certain occasions it is absolutely the right thing to do. It can be an enormous spiritual experience and a source of inspiration even in those dark days when I am harassed by utilization review nurses and the 1-800 number of the patient's insurance company.

Chapter 5

Prayer and the Five Senses: A Physician's Meditation

The physicians and nurses with whom I talk about spiritual matters often ask questions about how to pray. They want to know more about what prayer is and how to go about the practice of prayer, especially in the midst of their professional lives. Of course, there is no simple answer to their questions. Prayer is a many splendored thing. However, in this chapter, I would like to explore one approach that I think many clinicians might find helpful. It is not the only way in which I pray. But it is one way, and one way is better than no way.

Prayer has traditionally been defined as the lifting up to God of one's heart, mind, and soul. While this definition has been deemed adequate even by great twentieth century theologians,[1] I think there is something about it that is quite inadequate, especially as a definition of Christian prayer. Health care professionals in particular might notice that something is missing. The traditional definition ignores the role of the body in prayer. Heart and mind, in this definition, refer to our capacities for emotion and reason. They do not refer to the organ of circulation or the gray matter inside the round hollow of our skulls. But this inattention to the body implies a sort of dualism that *should* strike Christians as perplexing. After all, if we really do believe that God is active in the world and that God has loved us enough to become one of us, then it must seem all the more curious that the role of the body is missing from our definition of prayer.

We pray with our bodies. We have no choice in the matter. Even the traditional form of prayer called "mental prayer" ineluctably involves the body. One's body may be hot or cold, tired or energetic, young or old, fat or thin, sick or well. And all of this makes a difference. Prayer requires that one's body *be* somewhere. Somewhere may be a church, a car, an office, or the woods. Prayer also requires a certain degree of function in the central nervous system. As the apostles learned in the Garden of Gethsemane (Mt. 26:40–41), one must be alert (1 Pt. 5:8–9).

Prayers also take place *in* bodies. Genuine prayers involve all of us. When we really pray, we pray with our lymph and with our bones. Genuine prayer is something that gets underneath our fingernails like rich, black, fertile soil. We breathe prayer into our lungs like mountain air. We swim in it like water.

So I prefer to define prayer as the raising up to God of our entire selves—heart, mind, *body,* and soul. We cannot hold our bodies back from God, even in prayer. As St. Francis of Assisi has written, "Hold back nothing of your selves for yourselves, so that he who has given himself totally to you may receive you totally."[2] Every last tendon is God's.

The Five Senses

The idea that the body is important in prayer is not radical or new. It is obvious that the senses are involved in the life of prayer. St. Francis and St. Bonaventure and many great saints have been keenly aware of the role that the senses play in prayer. As St. Bonaventure writes, "Concerning the mirror of things perceived through sensation, we can see God not only through them as through vestiges, but also in them, as he is in them by his essence, power, and presence....We are led to contemplate God in all creatures which enter our minds through our bodily senses."[3] I do not mean to suggest that one cannot have a direct experience of God in prayer. I myself practice a form of prayer known as centering prayer, in which one attempts simply to be in the presence of God without attending to any particular sense experience. But even this form of prayer involves the body. A great deal of attention is focused on location, posture, and breathing. This sort of prayer is perfectly valid. Without effort of thought or "meditation" on a particular passage of scripture or any relationship to any particular sense experience, one can have genuine contact with God. This form of prayer can be very helpful for health care practitioners. Emptying the mind of the thoughts that preoccupy a busy clinician during the day can be exactly what the Great Physician orders, uncluttering the mind to make room for God. But in this chapter, I will offer a meditation on how God reaches people through the senses. And I believe this form of prayer will also be very useful for clinicians, whose job it is to make sense of sense experience on a daily basis.

Doctors and nurses, by virtue of their occupations, are keenly interested in the senses. They make use of all five of them in their daily work. Much of their work involves helping patients who have developed problems with the function of one or more of the senses. The clinician's work begins with symptoms. Symptoms are simply the strange things that patients sense, such as blurred vision, pain, an unusual taste, or ringing in the ears. Working as they do day in and day out with bodies, using their own five senses and asking patients about theirs, clinicians are immersed in a world of sense, a world inhabited by God. But how many clinicians have ever thought about the senses in relation to prayer? This question probably seems odd, but it strikes me as a problem that such a question should seem odd.

So I would like to invite the reader to come with me on a short spiritual journey through the senses—to think about God, prayer, and things spiritual in relation to the senses. Prayer is not a flight from the world. It is a journey into the depths of the world—a learning to relate to the world as God relates to the world. God made it all. And God saw that it was good (Gn. 1:3–31).

Smell

Smells have a way of evoking memories. Some have proposed that this is because the olfactory area of the brain is near the hippocampus, where it is believed that memory resides. Whatever the explanation, it is a recurrent human observation.

I discussed a bit about memory in relation to prayer in chapter 3. But in my previous discussion, I was referring to recent memories—for example, prayerfully remembering the patients one saw during the day. But the memories evoked by smell are much older. The odor of a certain food can, for example, remind one of one's grandmother. The fragrance of a certain flower may evoke memories of once having given that kind of flower to a certain special person or of having received one from such a person. Perhaps that special someone is now one's spouse of thirty years. Perhaps it was a long lost love.

The memories evoked by smell have an almost archeological character.

Medicine has its smells and memories as well. Many a physician, for example, decades later, will pass down a hallway in a medical center and suddenly smell an unmistakable odor that transports him or her back immediately to the first day of medical school. The smell of the preservatives for the cadavers of anatomy class is an unmistakable smell. Every time I smell it, I am reminded of that first incision right down the linea alba of the abdomen on the first day of medical school.

Smells in medicine have meaning in the present tense, as well as the past. The patient's breath may smell of alcohol or fetor hepaticus. A wound may smell of anaerobes. Blood in the gut has its own distinctive odor. And every good clinician knows by smell when he or she has entered a good nursing home or a bad nursing home—instantly.

The church also makes use of smell. Maybe I'd do well to join a church in the Orthodox tradition, because I don't think that we use enough incense in the Catholic Church. Incense connects me with some very significant moments in my life—moments when being in church was the occasion of deep religious experience. The smell of recently extinguished candles is also significant for me. It connects together a whole series of past events: birthday parties, the end of the Holy Thursday liturgy as the altar is stripped bare, Advent candles, and the clearing of the table after Thanksgiving dinner.

I do not intend this discussion as a mere exercise in nostalgia. Both the experience of these smells and the moments they evoke in memory can be genuine occasions of prayer. They need to be identified as such, claimed as such, cherished as such.

The time evoked by smell is the time of eternity. The time evoked by incense is God's time, not ours. If one is alert, the same can be true for the smell of the sea or the smell of fresh spring rain or the smell of alcohol on the breath of a patient who protests that he hasn't touched a drop. The time of eternity is the time of the God who was made man, who knows our finitude and our weakness. It is the time of the God who forgives us and nurtures us and knows how much we long for the infinite. God offers us moments of contact with eternity. God tells us that it's been there all along, right under our noses. In the words of the poet, "smell renews the salt savor of the sandy earth."[4] We inhale the grace of God.

Taste

"Taste and see how good the Lord is," declares the Psalmist. (Ps. 34:9). I'm afraid contemporary exegesis of this scriptural instruction is far too abstract. I think that we taste God in a more concrete fashion.

I will point out quickly that I am not suggesting that physicians return to the Hippocratic tradition of tasting urine to diagnose diabetes. I, for one, am only too happy to use a dipstick. But the spiritual meaning of the way the sense of taste operates in the lives of late twentieth century Americans is seriously underplayed.

The meaning of eating can be both bad and good. It seems to me, for instance, that one of the tell-tale signs of the problems in our society is the fact that, at least in Yuppie circles, there are no longer any sins except acts of dietary indiscretion. Sleeping around is not sinful. Insider trading is not sinful. Making nasty remarks about colleagues behind their backs is not sinful. *Chocolate cake* is sinful. *Ice cream* is decadent.

Contemporary culture is also experiencing, in the various health food kicks that are so popular today, a manifestation of a rather narcissistic desire to place the blame for everything that goes wrong with us outside of the person. This is coupled with a naive notion that immortality is the natural state of human beings. Disease, corruption, breakdown, weakness, and aging are not part of me as a human being. They come from without. I am not fallible. It is the world that corrupts me. I can avoid cancer if I eat a macrobiotic diet. I can live forever if I eat yogurt. Many of these food fads have nearly become religious cults. They manifest both the hunger so many people have for God and the rueful conviction that this hunger can be satisfied by eating vegetables.

The way a person relates to food tells a lot about how that person relates to the rest of the world. For instance, *why* a person eats is a serious question. For the vast majority of people on this planet, the answer is simple. They eat because they are hungry. But in America, things are different. Here, we eat because we are anxious. Eating and other sensual experiences become ways of attempting to fill up the sense of spiritual emptiness. The spiritual malaise of America is manifested in McDonalds as well as in the health food stores.

So some Americans stuff down hamburgers at their desks in order not to miss a moment of work. Others munch on junk food all day long. Still others cultivate the consumerism of experience. Among the privileged, it has now become gauche to strive to own a lot of expensive things. Instead, the new spirit of consumerism is to build up one's repertoire of experiences.

I do not wish to be misunderstood in making this claim. Traveling and eating out *can* be enriching experiences and times of profound sharing. But for some, these experiences can become ends in themselves. Many people pay all kinds of money to travel to the most exotic places. I think they're really looking for God. But instead, they brag about their time in Bali. Drug companies know that this is true of health care professionals. They send ads inviting them to conferences that are more about snorkeling than about congestive heart failure.

And the chic restaurants! I recently found myself in a restaurant with a few colleagues from my postdoctoral fellowship being asked, "How would you like your ostrich, sir?" No one had ever asked me *that* question before. One of my colleagues quipped, "He'd prefer it plucked." This was an outrageously overpriced restaurant that was really no place for a friar, but I have to confess that I liked it. Still, the comical nature of the waitress's question says something about me as an American.

Many Americans (and I do not exempt myself) are afflicted by the consumerism of experience. Americans pursue "lifestyles" of experience. While the object for many is to win the game of life by ending up with the most toys at the end, this is not the only kind of consumerism. For others, the object of the game is to win by ending up life having had the most experiences. So the object of life, for some of us, becomes trying to eat as many species as possible or to be able to put down others by saying smugly, "Been there. Done that." Frequently couples put off having children, for instance, not to solidify a marriage into which to welcome children or out of concern for overpopulation, but to preserve their precious "lifestyles."

In the meantime, most of the world is starving to death. In the meantime, the experience for which we really hunger, the experience of God, passes us by. God hungers for justice. As the poet, Pablo Neruda has written:

> Eating alone is a disappointment,
> but not eating matters more,
> is hollow and green, has thorns
> like a chain of fish hooks
> trailing from the heart,
> clawing at your insides.
>
> Hunger feels like pincers,
> like the bite of crabs,
> it burns, burns and has no fire.
> Hunger is a cold fire.
>
> For now I ask no more
> than the justice of eating.[5]

Our hunger for God hurts. And it cries out for satisfaction. Our hunger for justice also hurts. And it too cries out for satisfaction.

There is a sense in which the literal and the figurative hungers to which I refer are simply different aspects of the same hunger. We are called to attend to both aspects of the world's hunger—its hunger for God and its hunger for food. Yet the world in which we live is disordered. It can be characterized by the same maxim that is often used to describe the disordered biochemistry of diabetes—starvation in the midst of plenty. God asks for the justice of eating.

Eating is truly always a spiritual experience. But people need to rediscover this truth. Paradoxically, one way to do this is through fasting. Sometimes one needs to deprive oneself of something momentarily in order to appreciate it. Another way to recover this sense is through the old practice of eating in silence while on retreat. One gets to think about what food means before one eats. One learns to appreciate the taste of every morsel. One learns, through silent communion with the other silent retreatants, just how communal the act of sharing a meal really is, even without talking. That is why the old custom of saying grace before meals is so important to maintain. It is an important way to remind ourselves that God calls all people to join with all the holy ones in God's great messianic feast.

Food that is shared is holy. To taste such food is to taste the goodness of God. Jesus understood this. Admittedly, the church has so enervated the liturgical rites that it has been remarked that it is easier for Catholics to believe that the host we consume really is the body of Christ than it is to believe that it really is bread. But what we taste in the eucharist is the goodness of God. Taste the bread. Taste the wine. Know that Jesus meant it when he said, "For my flesh is real food, and my blood is real drink" (Jn. 6:55).

It would be difficult to underestimate the value of meals for the life of families. No professional career is worth as much to a health care professional or to his or her family as is this experience. Certainly, emergencies will call physicians and other health care professionals from the table to the hospital. But I would urge every health care professional *not* to make the hospital the routine for every meal. The family is a natural unit. The table is the natural sacrament of family life.

I do know the pressures families are under these days that threaten the sanctity of the supper table. Even the clergy and religious are not immune from these pressures. We friars experience these pressures as well. Everyone wants to hold their PTA meetings, Holy Name Society meetings, and liturgy committee meetings at 7 P.M. For health care professionals, the pressures are at least as great, and will only increase. HMOs want doctors and nurses to see patients as they come home from work, so that it will be more convenient for patients and the HMO can grab a greater market share. In addition, the children continue to belong to clubs, take piano lessons, and attend little league practices. I understand. I only want to urge a reassessment.

Every family can find its own time. Perhaps for some, it will be breakfast. Perhaps it will mean staking out one or two evenings a week in which evening activities are forbidden in favor of family time. Perhaps the local PTA could vote for such a day as a uniform school policy (*e.g.*, no evening meetings on Wednesdays). It is truly sacred time, to be nurtured and to be cherished. It is far more important to the spiritual development of parents and children than piano lessons or the HMO's market share.

Yet all meals are also sacrifices of sorts. Every meal has a host, and being a host always involves sacrifice. The mass is classically described as both a meal and a sacrifice. This is the official theological description offered by the church. There is no such thing as a free lunch. Jesus pays for this meal with his blood.

In the movie *Babette's Feast,* a bunch of very religious, but very somber, puritanical townsfolk, living in the dark, frigid winter of the Scandinavian north, are surprised to discover that the French woman who has lived among them as one in exile and disgrace for many years is capable of treating them one day, in a mad act of generosity, to an incredibly rich and delicious feast. To do this, she had to break out of her own self-pity and depression. She called upon wealthy friends from her former life to supply exotic ingredients to her small kitchen in this drab town. She worked on it to the point of exhaustion, giving of herself in preparing the meal. Nothing like it had ever occurred in the town. People came out of their private dwellings and encountered each other in a totally new way in the setting of the meal. Babette's feast changed their lives. Babette's generosity transformed them. This is the transformation promised by the God who in goodness and love sets the eucharistic table for Christians over and over again. Taste and see the goodness of God.

How deep, then, is the need for compassion toward those who cannot eat. When health care professionals care for patients suffering from esophageal cancer, for example, do they take the time to understand what this means? When hepatitis or chemotherapy or depression robs people of their sense of hunger, do clinicians countenance that suffering when making rounds? Or is the inability to eat just another clinical fact, a technological problem to be fixed by placement of a central venous line in the subclavian vein and the administration of Total Parenteral Nutrition?

One of my hematology professors was a very eccentric man. Among his eccentricities (or at least it seemed to me) was a preoccupation with his patients' eating habits. My fellow students and I used to want him to say more about pathophysiology or to demonstrate interesting diagnostic techniques at the bedside. Instead, he used to ask the patients, "Are you hungry?" He would take their untouched trays, open them up, take the spoon out of the plastic bag, and feed his patients himself. "Food is medicine," he used to say. "Eat some of this." He was right. And through him, I am convinced, many a patient was able to taste the goodness of God.

Touch

In the lobby of the Johns Hopkins Hospital in Baltimore, there is a huge, 10½-foot-tall marble statue of Christ, standing on a three-foot pedestal. Legend has it that when the hospital was first founded by Mr. Hopkins as a thoroughly secular institution, the wealthy religious people of the city were so scandalized that several of them conspired together to commission the sculpting of a statue of Christ as a "gift" to the new hospital. It was so big that once it arrived, it could only fit under the dome in the center of the main lobby. It was a gift that couldn't be turned down and couldn't be ignored.

Johns Hopkins is still a very secular institution, one that appears at times to worship the dome over the statue (the official symbol of its own greatness) much more than the figure that stands beneath it. The hospital's administrators are rather embarrassed by the statue to this day. They still don't know what to do with it. They now treat it as a historical piece: the administrators explain that this quaint artifact of a primitive mythological consciousness is part of an official, federally designated landmark building and therefore cannot be removed.

But the people who come to the hospital know what it's doing there. For over a century, patients and employees have been touching the right great toe of Jesus Christ as they enter the hospital. If one looks carefully, one notices that the marble toenail has become slightly worn. Like the woman with the hemorrhage who reached out from the crowd and touched the hem of the garment of Jesus

(Lk. 8:43–48), thousands of the sick and those who care for them have reached out to touch Jesus in the hope of being healed.

Health care professionals know the meaning of the laying on of hands, of how intimate their contact with their patients can be. The same phrase, "the laying on of hands," is used to describe the ordination of a priest. The power of God's presence can be felt by clinicians as the healing goes out from them. It can be felt by the patients who receive the healing touch. How human is this healing, and yet how divine.

But each person also knows of his or her own potential for spiritual numbness—for indifference to God and indifference to God's people. Health care professionals, especially, can get so caught up in the routine of work, so bored by the hypertensives and the diabetics and the somatizers, so angry about the government and the insurers, so cynical about their patients' inability to change, that they fail to recognize those moments in which power goes out of them. Perhaps, under such conditions, the power *has* failed to go out of them. If health care professionals do not encounter their patients as true persons, as unique children of God, they never really fully heal them. Perhaps the senses of contemporary clinicians are not as sharp as those of Jesus, who recognized the one who touched him as a real person, not just as one among a faceless crowd of sick, weak, fallible, complaining, needy people toward whom he was personally indifferent and unconcerned. Jesus needed no superhuman powers to do so. Jesus recognized her through his very human sense of touch. And that sense is open to every clinician today as well, as a portal through which God can enter their lives.

During the liturgy of the eucharist, one has the opportunity to touch those present through the sign of peace. It is an ancient gesture of the church, restored after the Second Vatican Council. It signals that one can find holiness if one does reach out and if one does touch one's brothers and sisters in a very real way. It is not just a handshake. In exchanging the sign of peace, Catholics really *do* exchange the love and the peace of Christ. It is not one's *own* well-wishes that one exchanges. It is the very love and the peace of Christ. Through touch.

And when patients are dying, do health care professionals

understand that they can communicate the grace of God through that same gentle touch? Too often the dying are abandoned. "There's nothing more we can do," say the physicians and nurses. They mutter something about being sorry, hang their heads, and walk away. But they can bring healing to the dying through touch, even when the disease is no longer curable.

The concept of healing is wider than the concept of curing. Health care professionals need to do everything they can to heal the fear and regret of their patients. They need to let the dying know that even as the bonds that connect them to the community of the living are in one sense dissolving, in another sense they remain closely connected to those who will remain and even to those who have gone before and those who are yet to come—connected through a network of compassion and love. Clinicians can do this through being there with their patients. They need write no orders. They need perform no tests. They need speak no words. A clasp of the hand will often be enough. Like the woman who touched the garment of Christ, and like the patients who touched the toe of the statue at Johns Hopkins, the sick look for healers. If Christian clinicians are healers, then they will know not just a faceless crowd of nobodies, but the embodied somebodies who have touched them. They will, in turn, be touched by the power of the Holy One.

Vision

All religions have stories of visions. And vision is critical to the work of health professionals as well. They observe breathing patterns and look through microscopes. They look at skin color and read EKG monitors.

It was only as a third-year medical student out on the wards for the first time that I began to realize that I could no longer get away with using my glasses only for seeing blackboards and slides projected on a screen. Once I was out on the wards of the hospital, I had to be able to look up rapidly from close work—writing in a chart, suturing, or other tasks—to be able to see things at a distance. The day the nurses were frantically pointing out a patient who needed my assistance, but I couldn't even see the patient because I had my glasses in my pocket while writing in a chart, was the day I learned about the importance of vision in the practice of medicine. Henceforth, I would wear glasses or contact lenses all the time.

Looking for visions is very human. Human beings seek the vision that will end all doubt and fear. Yet the spiritual life is often characterized by what St. John of the Cross called the "Dark Night of the Soul."[6] When every visual image one could ever want seems to be instantly available through television, the VCR rental store, or the Internet, people have little patience for such Dark Nights. They look for instant gratification. As in the time of Jesus, the present age not only asks for, but demands, signs (Mt. 12:39; 16:4; Mk. 8:12; Lk. 11:29), and demands them instantly. I suspect that there are at least some who have tried to pray, but have given up in disappointment when, after having seated themselves in a church for ten whole minutes, not a single vision occurred. In part, this is because they have confused prayer with magic in much the same way that they have confused healing with magic. Genuine religious experience is not something that one can conjure up. Prayer is not scripted by the authors of *I Dream of Jeanie.*

But neither is mystical experience simply a matter for experts. It is not reserved for priests, monks, and nuns. The divine spark is in each of us. Each human being is a temple for the Holy Spirit. All people are natural mystics. But they are not magicians. The moment one tries to force God to give one a mystical vision, one obliterates the possibility that it will ever happen. Prayer is about letting God show human beings the way.

Prayer is often only the experience of waiting. Prayer is sometimes nothing more than the conscious experience of desire for God. It might not even be a sense of the presence of God. It might be only darkness and silence. But this is not because God does not listen or because God doesn't care. It happens because human beings are so blind that it takes a long time to learn to see. But each human being will come to see God if he or she persists. God promises sight to the blind.

When Jesus chastises the Pharisees who see the specks in their brothers' and sisters' eyes but cannot see the planks in their own, remember that the message is directed to all people in every age (Lk. 6:37–42). Health care professionals, particularly doctors, are very good at picking out specks from the eyes of others, but inept at seeing the plank in their own. Health care professionals are often very harsh on patients, but expect patients to be very understanding when, for example, the physician is late in arriving somewhere. Perhaps this is why the longest section in the Gospels on the topic of judgmentalism is written by Luke the physician. God invites health care professionals to see themselves clearly so that God might heal them in their blindness. All that is required is that they admit that they are blind in the first place.

We all have our blind spots, don't we? Prayer is the practice of focusing the light of truth on ourselves and on our world. It is about seeing ourselves and others and the world around us more clearly. As St. Francis once admonished his followers, "What we are before God, that we are, and nothing more."[7]

Prayer sharpens vision. It is like the difference between the intern and the attending physician examining the patient. When the attending has the ophthalmoscope in hand, it is the attending who sees the Roth spot and confirms the diagnosis of subacute bacterial endocarditis. When praised by the intern, the attending says, "It was easy. My eyes are no sharper than yours. The difference between your exam and mine was that I knew what I was looking for."

There will be moments of sudden illumination for everyone, eventually, if one keeps at it. But these moments come on God's time, not human time. Prayer is not like TV. The praying person does not control the horizontal. The praying person does not control the vertical. There is no remote control device. As the poet, T.S. Eliot, puts it,

> I said to my soul, be still, and wait without hope
> For hope would be hope for the wrong thing; wait without love
> For love would be love of the wrong thing; there is yet faith
> But the faith and the hope and the love are all in the waiting.
> Wait without thought, for you are not ready for thought:
> So the darkness shall be the light, and the stillness the dancing.[8]

One can make effective use of the visual in one's experience of prayer. God speaks to human beings through mountain vistas and sunsets over the ocean and moonlight glittering on freshly fallen snow. Icons and other paintings of saints or of Christ can help to focus prayers, reminding each person that holiness occurs in the flesh and that by seeing holiness in others, one can seek after it oneself. The statues, crucifixes, stained glass, and candles of churches also help. Christians need not worry about idolatry. As Bonaventure reminds us, "The creatures of the sense world signify the invisible attributes of God."[9] What one sees can help in one's effort to lift oneself up to God entirely—heart, mind, body, and soul.

And if one perseveres, God will correct all our distorted self-images and let us see clearly in the mirror of truth. God promises that this truth will set us free (Jn. 8:32).

Hearing

In some very fundamental ways, prayer is about listening. Health care professionals are woefully neglectful about listening. Studies have shown that physicians interrupt their patients, on average, within 18 seconds of their initial words.[10] Richard Baron relates a wonderful story about a physician who was paying careful attention to a heart murmur, taking the stethoscope off the chest of a patient who had begun to say something and scolding, "Shhhhh. I can't hear you while I'm listening."[11] As with our patients, so it is with our God.

One can shut others out either by concentrating exclusively on what one wants to do for oneself, or by constantly talking about oneself and one's own concerns and never letting others have their say. As it is written in the book of Ecclesiastes:

> Words from the wise man's mouth win favor but the fool's lips consume him. The beginning of his words is folly, and the end of his talk is utter madness; Yet the fool multiplies words. (10:12-14)

The multiplication of words is a particular problem for those who are in academic health care settings, especially academic physicians. The publish-or-perish frenzy has become absurd. The volume of medical literature is huge and is growing bigger all the time. But I really wonder how much of this verbiage is worth anything at all.

The multiplication of words is also an occupational hazard for clergy and religious. I guess this means I am at double jeopardy—or rather, that whoever reads a book written by a friar-physician is at double jeopardy. Religious often spend too much time talking or too much time preparing fine words for others that they do not bother to try to incorporate into their own lives. It is very easy to shut out God by talking about religion. Shhhh. I can't hear you while I'm listening.

That is why silence can be so good for Americans. It is so hard to find silence in our world. People run from it. They block it out with televisions and compact disks. But Americans, in some ways, are usually drowning out God, the very one they really want to hear. God must ponder human behavior, musing with the words of the poet, Ezra Pound, "She would like some one to speak to her,/ and is almost afraid that I/ will commit that indiscretion."[12]

Silences vary in their particular qualities. The qualities of a particular silence depend on the place and also on the state of mind of the one who goes into the silence. Monasteries are generally good places to find silence. I still carry with me an incredible memory of a very cold February morning, well before dawn, walking to lauds at a Benedictine abbey in rural Vermont. It was so dark that I could barely see anything as I walked along the road from the guest house to the chapel, except the dim light from the abbey in the distance. There was no wind, and just a few very large, silent flurries fell around me. My shoes squeaking against the snow were the only sound. I must have stopped twenty times in a quarter mile just to hear the silence. In this silence I heard God saying, over and over, "Be still and confess that I am God! I am exalted among the nations, exalted on the earth" (Ps. 46:10).

God speaks to us from the silences of our own hearts. When we are troubled in spirit, all those demons that we have denied exist within us, the personal demons that we have tried to ignore, start to speak. God offers his healing to us in these silences. All of us are haunted, from time to time, by unclean spirits that shriek loudly when we enter into silence and invoke the name of God. "What do you want of us, Jesus of Nazareth? Have you come to destroy us?"(Mk. 1:24) Jesus will heal us if we let him. But sometimes such painful silences are necessary in order for us to recognize the demons that possess us and to ask God to expel them.

The word of God enters through our ears. Sometimes this happens when we listen to other people and their needs. It happens when health care professionals hear the symptoms of their patients, not merely as clinical data, but as real pain and real suffering. It happens when Christian clinicians really listen to their patients as human beings listening to human beings. Incredible things will begin to happen in the health care system if clinicians start listening with this kind of care. Physicians and nurses will begin to hear the voice of God. They will hear the voice of the one who cries out from the cross, "My God, my God, why have you forsaken me?" (Mt. 27:46). They will begin to hear the voice of the one who proclaims, "I am the way, and the truth, and the life" (Jn. 14:6). They will begin, in the very midst of their practices, to hear the words of eternal life. And like Peter, they will confess that they have nowhere else to go but to follow the one who speaks to them (Jn. 6:68–69).

Prayer will make all people better listeners. One can learn to hear echoes of the songs of the heavenly chorus when one hears hymns at mass. God invites everyone to do more than listen to this music. All those present are invited to join their voices with those of the choir. The careful listener hears God's word proclaimed in the midst of the assembly. The careful listener hears the words of the eucharistic prayer, not as priestly mumbo-jumbo, but as God's prayer for everyone. The careful listener learns to hear the needs of family and neighbors. The careful listener learns to hear the cry of the poor (Ps. 69:34). And careful clinicians can learn to hear what their patients are *really* trying to say, not just what they want or expect their patients to say.

The Prayer of the Five Senses

So I pray with all people, all men and women with bodies, who know and experience so much through the five senses, asking that God will bless the wonderful neuronal structures with which we have been endowed and will enable us to find and know the Holy One through these senses. We lift up our senses to God, along with our hearts, minds, souls, and bodies—with all that we are. May everything within us give thanks and praise to God.

> *We thank you, O God, for the wonder of smell, and ask that our prayers rise up to you like a sweet oblation of incense (Ps. 141:2). We thank you, O God, for the gift of taste, for you feed us with the finest wheat, and you are sweeter than honey from the rock (Ps. 81:17). We thank you, O God, for the gift of touch, and pray that we might touch you and know that you are not a ghost, but living flesh (Lk. 24:39). We thank you, O God, for the gift of vision, for we know that you are the light of the world (Jn. 8:12) and that you give sight to us in our blindness (Lk. 4:18). And we thank you, O God, for the gift of hearing, for we know that we are truly blest when we hear your word and keep it (Lk. 11:28). Make our senses keen that we may know you and know your love for us and that we may serve you and serve your people. Through Christ, our Risen Savior. Amen.*

Chapter 6

Suffering, Spirituality, and Health Care

There are those who say that the only proper responses to human suffering are to relieve it, where possible, or otherwise to remain silent. People who suffer, it is said, want either relief or consolation. They do not want lectures.

There is much truth to such remarks. But clinicians know the simple reality that relief is not always possible and that consolation is not always immediately apparent. In the face of this, is mute silence all there is to consolation?

A series of reflections on spirituality in health care would seem radically incomplete without *some* direct discussion of suffering. The theme of suffering has been lurking just beneath the surface of much of what has already been discussed in this book. The theme of suffering is unavoidable in any serious discussion of spirituality and health care.

Everyone who cares for the sick sees human suffering every day. All who are serious about reflecting on what they are doing in health care are compelled to search somehow for the meaning of that suffering. Once a health care professional ceases such soul-searching, I should think that person counted among the most inhuman members of the species. But sadly, I suspect the number of physicians and nurses who reflect regularly and seriously on the meaning of suffering is small.

I must also note at the outset how paradoxical I find it that people today seem completely unwilling to accept any rational explanation for suffering, yet reject religion precisely because it cannot seem to provide one. I will make no pretenses in this chapter of offering any such rational explanation of suffering. I will not engage in any systematic *theology* of suffering *(theodicy)*. What I will offer in these pages is a spiritual *reflection* on human suffering and the practice of the health care professions.

Physicians, nurses, pastoral care staff, medical social workers, and other health care professionals routinely witness the suffering of others. I will not try to explain why this must be so, or why a loving God should allow men and women to suffer in all of the myriad ways that health care professionals know better than anyone else. But a discussion of spirituality and the experience of suffering is absolutely necessary for a spirituality of health care. In a very real way, it may be said that if suffering has no spiritual meaning, then no spirituality of health care is possible.

Pain and Suffering

Suffering must be distinguished from pain. Not all suffering is caused by pain and not all pain causes suffering. Pain is a physiological phenomenon. It results from the stimulation of certain types of nerve cells. Pain experts teach that pain signals can be distinguished into three basic types—somatic, visceral, and neuropathic. Somatic pains are from the surface of the body, visceral pains are from inside, and neuropathic pains are due to damage to nerves themselves. Psychologists and pain experts also classify pain on the basis of duration into acute and chronic. These distinctions should be readily apparent and meaningful for every clinician, but they are specifications of a variety of experiences that human beings share with most multicellular animals.

Pain is also affected by the psychological milieu in which it is experienced (something that human beings also share, to some extent, with animals). For example, it is well known that different ethnic groups have different experiences of identical painful stimuli.[1] Pain signals undergo enormously complex cognitive processing. Despite the fact that there appear to be only three basic types of pain, human beings classify their experiences of pain in rather remarkable ways—as sharp, dull, burning, aching, crampy, pressure, hankering, gnawing, and the like. And the duration of pain seems to make a difference. Acute pain that is over quickly is dealt with quite differently from pain that is of a lower level of intensity but never goes away.

Suffering, on the other hand, is something very different from pain. Suffering has less to do with the stimulation of pain fibers than it does with the experience of persons. What I mean by this is something far different from a comment about the cognitive processing of pain signals in some very broad sense. Suffering is experienced in relation to one's situation in life. One can experience pain without suffering, as an athlete in training might experience the pain of exertion toward a new limit of physical endurance, but not understand this to be suffering. Or, one can suffer without experiencing pain, as when marital discord causes immense suffering without the slightest bit of physical pain. The field of suffering is wider than pain, wider than sickness, wider even than death. As John Paul II has remarked, "What we express by the word *suffering* seems to be particularly essential to the nature of human beings."[2]

Suffering and Being Human

If suffering has more to do with the nature of being human than it does with pain per se, it follows that one must understand what it means to be human in order to understand what it means to suffer. While such a statement may seem simple, it is, in fact, very significant. To understand what it means to suffer, one must understand what it means to be human. No wonder, then, that suffering has been called a mystery. It is as deep a mystery as being human.

Even when the entire sequence of the human genome has been elucidated, only the most foolish of scientists will dare to suggest that he or she thereby has explained what it means to be human. Likewise, no one will ever be able to identify the tracks along which "suffering fibers" travel in the central nervous system, or identify the "suffering area" of the brain. The body has pain centers, but there are no suffering centers. There could be no such thing. Suffering is not a part of the brain. It is a part of the mystery of being human.

Some have thought that a distinction between merely being alive and being a *person* is a useful distinction in discussions of suffering, asserting that it is only persons who suffer. Prominent among these authors is Dr. Eric Cassell, who has offered a list of the characteristics that he suggests define a person. From this list, he proceeds to discuss suffering. Among the characteristics he lists as necessary ingredients for personhood are memory, relationships, personality, having a body, being aware of the future, and being oriented to the transcendent.[3]

This is not a bad list, and I deeply admire Cassell's work. But it seems to me that this sort of list leaves open the danger that some members of the human family won't measure up to Cassell's definition of a person. I think that such a list is better thought of as a list of potential spheres of human suffering. For example, if I lose my memory, on Cassell's theory I become less human. That would seem to imply that I would be less prone to suffering. But this seems wrong. It seems to me that in such a situation I would suffer greatly as a human person who has lost his memory. Similarly, in a real way, I would suffer if I were to enter into a permanent coma, even though I might be unaware of relationships or of the future, unable to express a personality, and robbed of memory in a purgatory that would leave me unable to pass over into the transcendent. If only persons suffer, and if to be a person is to have all of the characteristics on Cassell's list, then human beings in permanent comas would not be persons and could not be thought to suffer. But most people would say that there is a real sense in which a person who is in a permanent coma is suffering. A person in a permanent coma might not feel pain, but it still makes sense to say that such a person is suffering. The characteristics mentioned in lists like Cassell's had best not be looked upon as necessary characteristics for membership in the personhood "club." They are all characteristics of normal species functioning for human beings and spheres in which human beings can suffer. But it is not necessary to be possessed of *all* of these characteristics in order to be human. And it is not necessary that one or all of these characteristics should be functioning normally in order to say that a human being is suffering. To understand suffering, it is necessary to understand what it means to be human. No short list will tell anyone what it means to be human.

Human Being and the Transcendent

Two characteristics from Cassell's list are, if understood from a spiritual perspective, definitely constitutive of the human. These are not themselves sufficient to *define* the human, but they are the only two characteristics on Cassell's lists that are truly necessary. These two essential characteristics are (1) the fundamental orientation of the human species toward the transcendent, and (2) the fact that being human always means being-in-relationship. All human beings share these characteristics in radical equality, regardless of any personal powers, talents, characteristics, or circumstances. No human beings will ever lack these characteristics, no matter what should befall them. Further, these characteristics do not admit of degrees. One cannot have more or less of them.

In some ways, these two characteristics are two sides of the same coin. Understood in an explicitly religious sense, since God is the ultimate term of transcendence, orientation toward the transcendent and being in relationship with God are simply different ways to express the same phenomenon.

The relationship to the transcendent is already a given in human existence, albeit in an implicit or "prethematic" manner. And although conscious experience is not necessary in order to have this relationship, this relationship is a precondition for conscious experience. Certainly it is true that human beings can have direct access to the transcendent through religious experience, identified as such. But those who would deny that they have religious experience, as I said in chapter 1, cannot deny any and all experience of the transcendent. This experience of transcendence comes to human beings through intellectual, moral, and aesthetic experiences, as well as through explicitly religious experiences.

To recognize any limit is to know that there is something beyond that limit. To know finitude is to know the infinite. And this is knowledge of the transcendent, even if it is never named as religious experience.

Human beings understand horizons. Visibility, for example, has its limits. But to recognize a limit implies that one knows of existence beyond the limit. Even to ask a question is to recognize an intellectual limit. To know death is to recognize a limit as well.

Human beings also know evil. And this knowledge is only possible if one has an understanding of another transcendental category—the good. To know evil, one must know the good. To recognize injustice, one must know justice. Human beings may argue a great deal about what the good *is,* or about whether this or that particular state of affairs is just, or what this implies for human behavior. But all seem to acknowledge that there are such things as good and evil, just and unjust. And they seem to want to strive beyond the limits of evil. The quest for the good is a quest for ultimacy, a quest for the transcendent.

Human beings also know beauty. They can recognize the inherent unity that emerges from the particularity and diversity of a set of paint marks on a canvas. They recognize in Michelangelo's *David* something more than a hunk of marble—more, even, than the representation of a man in the marble. Such knowledge is possible only if one has had an experience of the transcendent. Arguments abound about exactly what is worthy of the descriptive adjective *beautiful,* but no one denies that there are such things as ugliness and beauty. Human beings create works of art, write symphonies, and sculpt statues. Human beings do not create works of art simply to enhance the mating process or to warn of approaching predators. Human beings seek the ultimacy of the beautiful.

All of these experiences of the ultimate *can* be ways to experience the transcendence of God. Genuine religious experience may be had either through direct experience of God or through an intellectual, moral, or aesthetic experience that culminates in the ultimacy of God. But even those who would deny the experience of God cannot deny the experience of ultimacy.

Human Being and Relationship

In Jewish and Christian thought, each and every human being is created in the image and the likeness of the transcendent God. Human beings are defined much more by this relationship with God than by any particular powers that one or another member of the species exercises. This is what gives human beings their dignity.

I frequently make the mistake, when typing, of reversing the positions of the 'l' and the 'a' in the word *relationship.* What appears on the page is "realtionship." I actually find this mistake instructive. Sounding out the mistake I repeatedly make suggests that relationship is "real sonship." For human beings, to be real is to be in relationship. To be real is to be a child of God, to be in relationship with God. This being-in-relationship with God is ineradicable. Human beings can ignore it in themselves or in others. They can reject it in themselves or in others. But they cannot destroy it. It is already a given in every human situation.

Human beings are also in special relationship with each other. Being human *means* being in relationship with other human beings. And if one takes seriously the revealed truth that all human beings are created in the image and likeness of God, then one will readily understand that all human relationships reflect the one fundamental relationship that each human being has with God. This is the truth expressed by John Donne in his famous meditation: "No man is an island, entire of itself. Each is a part of the main, a piece of the whole. If a clod should be washed into the sea, Europe is the less."[4]

Thus the value or dignity of being human is not the Hobbesian notion that this is "his Price—that is to say, so much as would be given for the use of his Power: and therefore is not absolute, but a thing dependent upon the need and judgment of another."[5] Ultimate human dignity does not change with market conditions. Every human being is a child of God, made in the image and the likeness of God. The dignity of the human is based on this relationship with God as Father and, consequently, with all other human beings as brothers and sisters, equally children of the one God.

Suffering and Finitude

Taking everything that I have written thus far together, I want to offer one simple insight into the spiritual meaning of suffering. I am not offering an explanation of suffering. I am not trying to explain *why* people suffer. I am simply making a suggestion about what it means to suffer. My suggestion is this: All suffering may be understood, in its root form, as the experience of finitude. Human beings are fundamentally oriented toward the infinite term of transcendence, yet aware that everything about them is radically limited. Human beings are oriented toward the truth, yet plagued by their nature as fallible, ignorant, and prone to make choices that are opposed to the truth—lying, cheating, deceiving, and exaggerating their greatness. Human beings are oriented toward the good, yet live in a world plagued by physical evils, such as pain and disease, and prone to make choices of hatred, bigotry, and selfishness. Human beings are oriented toward the beautiful, yet aware that they are not themselves totally beautiful, that they all grow old, that their beauty fades, and that they are prone to make choices of the ugly and to disfigure each other and the world. Human beings are oriented toward infinite freedom, yet live in a world in which choices are severely constrained by nature and are prone to make choices that enslave themselves and others. Human beings are oriented toward the infinite, yet live in a world that is finite. They lead lives that are marked by ineluctable death and make choices that lead to finitude and to death, sometimes even killing each other and killing themselves.

Suffering is part of the nature of being human. Suffering is the experience that human beings have of knowing themselves as finite creatures who have been given the gift of a freedom that orients them to the infinite. Human beings are susceptible to suffering every time they make a choice, because to choose one thing is to give up something else. Every free choice is therefore a reminder of finitude. And to be reminded of finitude is to suffer.

Human beings are also susceptible to suffering whenever they experience pain, because pain has a way of focusing their attention on their vulnerability, making them aware of some threat to their existence, or of some rent in their bodily integrity that foreshadows the day of dissolution. Chronic pain has a way of engendering worse suffering than acute pain because the reminder of finitude is constant, not short-lived. Every pain is a reminder of finitude. And to be reminded of finitude is to suffer.

Human beings are also susceptible to suffering when their choices are constrained and controlled, because to lose control is to be reminded of one's radical insufficiency and radical dependence upon God. To be under the control of others or of natural processes outside one's will is to be reminded of one's finitude. And to be reminded of finitude is to suffer.

Finally, human beings suffer whenever they become ill because all illness smells of death, mortality, and finitude. Illness imposes limits. Illness causes pain. Those who are ill always lose some measure of control. To be ill is to be reminded of one's finitude. And to be reminded of one's finitude is to suffer.

Suffering and Health Care

The suffering of the sick and the dying is perhaps the most basic form of suffering. This is the true etymology of the word, *patient*. It is from the Latin, *patiens,* 'one who suffers.' Every cough, every drop of blood, every wave of nausea is a reminder of finitude. Finitude is the message, and illness is the messenger.

Understanding this may help physicians and nurses in caring for patients. It may help to avert the judgmentalism of those who would complain that their patients are exaggerating their symptoms or bothering them with trivial concerns. After all, whether the patient's back pain is caused by a pulled muscle, a slipped disc, depression, or metastatic cancer, the patient, one of the not yet dead, is being reminded that the day of death is coming. On the cosmic scale, then, the significance of each patient's back pain is exactly the same. Whether it is caused by depression or by cancer, back pain implies finitude. It still evokes for each patient, in some very real way, the mystery of death.

In another sense, however, to say that the patient's suffering is a mystery is not helpful in the concreteness of daily clinical practice. What does it mean to say that suffering is a mystery? If it only means that it is something that cannot be explained, this is hardly an explanation.

I would like to avoid thinking of God as merely the answer to the questions for which I have no good reply. As I insisted in chapter 2, God is not a stop-gap for incomplete knowledge. The mystery of suffering can only be understood in terms of the mystery of being human. Being human inevitably involves being in relationship with the transcendent, being oriented to the transcendent, and yet possessing a knowledge of radical incompleteness and finitude. Can anything more be gleaned from this insight that might help clinicians, especially Christian clinicians, to understand and to respond to the suffering of their patients?

Sympathy, Empathy, and Compassion

Everyone, as a potential patient, experiences symptoms. If they persist, or have a certain magnitude or quality, the one who is suffering (perhaps with the aid of family and friends) comes to recognize the significance of these symptoms and assumes the sick role (*i.e.*, becomes sick). Further persistence or intensity or worry may lead next to consultation with a health care professional—a nurse, a physician's assistant, or a physician. This is how the sick person becomes a patient.

Health care professionals recognize that their patients suffer from diseases. A disease is a relatively objectified categorization of the patient's subjective experience of physical suffering that is recognized as such by professionals. Clinicians classify the physical occasions of suffering and have a scientific understanding of these physical occasions. But understanding the *physical* occasion of the patient's suffering does not mean understanding the patient's suffering. The suffering of another can never be fully known. Still, this does not mean that the suffering of a patient cannot be known at all, or that suffering is wholly private.

At the very least, a health care professional can approach the patient (the one who suffers) with sympathy. Sympathy is a state in which one feels distressed by the distress of others. Physicians, nurses, or other clinicians themselves can feel bad that the patient feels bad. This is sympathy, and it is a very good thing. But a good clinician will be more than sympathetic.

The good clinician is empathetic. The empathetic clinician is the one who says to the patient, "I think I can appreciate how you feel." Genuine empathy is the attempt to understand the suffering of the patient as the *patient* experiences it. This is at least partially possible, and it would certainly represent a step in the right direction for all health care professionals. But ultimately, even empathy will be insufficient. What is necessary is true compassion.[6]

True compassion is the most complete response that a clinician can have toward a patient. The compassionate health care professional engages the suffering of the patient at three levels. First, the compassionate clinician is the one who objectively recognizes the suffering of the patient, giving it a name and understanding its natural history. Second, the compassionate clinician is the one who subjectively responds to this suffering with feelings of genuine empathy for the patient, striving to understand the situation of the patient as experienced by the patient. Third, the compassionate clinician is the one who is moved to concrete healing actions—words and deeds. Compassion is always active, even if these actions are no more than kind words and a gentle touch. This is the spirit of true Samaritanism. God's life suffuses the compassionate response to suffering that characterizes all true acts of healing. It is through compassion that God is made manifest in the relationship between clinician and patient.

Being Human: Love and Suffering

I will state it again: To understand the meaning of suffering, one must understand the meaning of being human. Suffering is an ineluctable part of the human condition. Just as all human beings will die, all human beings will suffer. To live a life characterized by a denial of the existence of suffering, or a life of constant effort to escape suffering, is to live a life of delusion.

The philosopher of religion John Hick asks those who would deny this fact to try to imagine a world without suffering.[7] Imagine a world in which no one who was ever shot, run over by a car, or fell from a ladder ever suffered any pain, injury, or death. Such a world would be very strange. It would be a world devoid of heroes, for instance, because there would never be any danger and therefore there would never be anyone in need of rescue. Or imagine a world in which a thief could steal a million dollars without anyone suffering the loss of a penny of it. Such a world would be absurd. Good and evil would cease to be categories by which to judge the fruits of human interactions. No one could ever possibly be wronged. Mercy would have no meaning. Justice would have no point.

In fact, it is not hyperbole to say that there is no love without suffering. To paraphrase the First Letter of John, "anyone who says that he or she loves, and does not suffer, is a liar."

Once again, I am not attempting to explain *why* anyone suffers. I am only acknowledging the fact that people do suffer and that physicians, nurses, and other clinicians are involved firsthand in this fact every day. Clinicians are not specially equipped to deal with suffering in ways that other human beings are not. They can treat pain and disease and a few other medical conditions that *cause* suffering, but they cannot treat suffering itself. There are no pills to treat suffering. Suffering is not a symptom. It is part of the mystery of being human. Clinicians have no direct therapy for suffering. They can only respond with human compassion toward those who are suffering, treating those conditions that give rise to suffering acutely or chronically. But when medicine, a finite art, meets its limits, all the clinician can do is to be compassionately present.

To be compassionate is to be fully human. As a finite creature oriented toward the infinite, I can only transcend my own finitude by reaching out actively, beyond the limits of my individual existence, to touch the infinite in a fellow finite creature. When I am compassionate, I transcend my own finitude and reach the infinite in the suffering other. This is where the infinite orientation of my humanity points—toward the limitless, uncharted sea of compassionate love.

This is why God, in his compassion, *had* to become human. God's infinity had to know the suffering of human finitude and still reach out beyond it to embrace the infinite orientation of his suffering creatures. Jesus understood the necessity of walking down this path no better than we do. He asked that the cup pass him by. In the end, he recognized that it could not.

Thus, I have faith that God can be found in the midst of the suffering that is the stock and trade of health care. I struggle to understand it. I am certain that I cannot explain it.

Compassion is a manifestation of love. And love, whatever else it may be, is something that involves choices. Love is the one true source of freedom in the midst of the suffering human finitude entails. Choosing between options is a condition of freedom in finitude. Every free choice involves suffering. To say yes to love involves saying no to something else. One cannot both help the homeless man who has had a seizure on the street where one is walking and get to the grocery store before it closes. One cannot be charitable toward anyone without giving something—time, effort, money, or something else. But this is the true paradox of compassionate love. By making the choice to love and facing the suffering and the finitude that love requires, one transcends finitude and embraces the ultimate freedom of boundless love.

God does not want *anyone* to suffer for the sake of suffering. But no one can avoid suffering altogether. And to make the fulfillment of one's own plans the central theme of one's life is to try to avoid the finitude, suffering, and lack of control that compassion and love demand. No physician or nurse is worthy of the name Christian if he or she continually shrinks from the suffering that compassion and love demand in response to the suffering of others. Such suffering is not a test from God, but only the simultaneous embracing of the human condition and the choice to love.

God gives everyone the freedom to choose as well as the knowledge both that life involves choices and that choices involve suffering. Love calls forth compassionate responses to the suffering of others. Only choices that are made in love can transcend that suffering.

Suffering and Salvation

Suffering, one's own and that of others, can be the occasion of salvation. If one suffers and in that suffering experiences limitation and finitude but still manages to hold out hope for the infinite, faith in what lies beyond the horizon, and love for the God who calls everyone forth into his marvelous light (1 Pt. 2:9), one is on the road to salvation. This is the way Jesus has shown. As St. Paul has written:

> We are afflicted in every way, but not
> constrained; perplexed, but not driven to despair;
> persecuted, but not abandoned; struck down,
> but not destroyed; always carrying about in
> the body the dying of Jesus, so that the life of Jesus
> may also be manifested in our bodies. (2 Cor. 4:8–11)

To relieve the suffering of another is also an occasion of salvation. But this cannot be done just with medicines. Medical treatment can eliminate some of the causes of suffering by forestalling the moment of death or by restoring some functional freedoms, but only compassionate love can overcome suffering itself. Suffering means finitude and limitation. Love means infinity and freedom. Just as Jesus did not ignore the woman who reached out to him from the faceless crowd of needy people and touched him (Lk. 8:40–48), so too, health care professionals who claim to follow him cannot ignore the suffering of their patients. Christian health care professionals have a special responsibility to care for the needs of the sick, whom they have pledged to serve. Treating diseases and managing symptoms is not enough. Suffering is not a disease or a symptom and cannot be cured or eliminated by medicine. Suffering is only healed through compassionate love. In imitating the healing work of Christ, Christian clinicians enter more deeply into the kingdom of God. In following the example of the Good Samaritan, they heal with the wine of fervent zeal and with the oil of compassion.

But they are also called to humility. Medicine does not have an answer for all causes of suffering, not even all suffering of a physical nature. Medicine today does an incredibly good job of treating pain. Innovations such as the simultaneous use of multiple kinds of adjuvant pain medicines, the administration of narcotics through patches on the skin, nerve blocks, continuous infusions of medicines into the spinal fluid, and patient controlled analgesia, in which patients can give themselves (within safe limits) extra doses of narcotics in addition to a continuous baseline infusion, are all wonderful. But they are not perfect. Most, but not all pain can be controlled. But even if it could, not all suffering is caused by pain. Feelings of fear, loneliness, embarrassment, helplessness, hopelessness, and abandonment are all aspects of suffering that morphine does not touch.

Nonetheless, health care professionals can still be healers in situations dominated by these sorts of suffering. Healing, in such situations, consists in the acknowledgment of the reality of the suffering, in expressions of empathy and compassion, in silent presence, and in the process of reminding the patient that he or she still has intrinsic dignity, still has meaning and value, even in the midst of dependency and fear. Genuine healing requires compassion. Only through compassion can one touch the infinite in the suffering other.

In a Christian context, one can appreciate that it is no accident that many of the great saints have had profound experiences of God in the midst of immense personal suffering. I, for my own part, sometimes think that I ought to take off my shoes before entering the room of a patient who is facing death with real faith, hope, and love. As a physician, I find such experiences to be encounters with the Holy.

John Paul II has written of the virtue of perseverance in the face of suffering. He writes,

> in doing this, the individual unleashes hope, which maintains in him the conviction that suffering will not get the better of him, that it will not deprive him of his dignity as a human being, a dignity linked to the awareness of the meaning of life.[8]

Suffering is only possible for creatures that have dignity and that search for meaning.

Suffering, Christ, and Health Care

The Gospels do not offer a neat theological answer to the problem of suffering. All that the Gospels offer is Christ himself as an example. Once again: To understand the mystery of suffering requires an understanding of the human. Suffering is part of being human. God's understanding of human suffering reaches a complete expression in the suffering of Jesus, who, as fully human, suffers like any and every other human being. In Jesus, God understands our suffering from the inside out. Jesus in the Garden of Gethsemane is the God who sweats with us, bleeds with us, suffers with us. Jesus at Golgotha is the God who dies for us and ultimately rises for us. There simply *is* no resurrection without the cross. In Jesus, God takes on the limitations of human finitude and transcends them through divine love. He shows us the path. The way of truth and life laid out for us passes through Gethsemane and Golgotha.

Health care professionals can make the Way of the Cross every day. They see patients live out their own unique passion plays, subsumed under the passion of Christ. They see patients unjustly condemned to painful diagnoses. They see them scorned, misunderstood, unable to continue their work, abandoned, and even mocked for their infirmities. They see them fall and get up, fall and get up, and fall and get up again and again and again. They see them take up huge crosses that they do not deserve. They see people who seem to come out of nowhere to help them. They see the women, always the women, who attend to the most basic needs of the dying in their final hours and days. They hear the dying cry out in prayers of warning for all the living. They dumbly witness the physical pains of patients that sometimes seem to tear muscle and nerve away from bone. They see patients who seem fixed somewhere between earth and heaven, hanging there for what seems to be an eternity. They offer unctions that can sometimes seem as effective in the face of all this as vinegar and hyssop. They are often among those left standing, when it is finally finished, in blood and water and tears, offering faint comfort to family and friends. They send the bodies away to be anointed and buried.

But if they can see Christ in every patient's Golgotha, if they can understand that hope has more to do with the human spirit than it does with prognostication,[9] if they can see the resurrection that is promised for all who suffer in love, they will know that God is with them in their work. I pray that such insight might come to all those physicians and nurses who are confused by the suffering of their patients, fearful, and disenchanted with their work. It may be that they will learn this from some ordinary man or woman with as ordinary an occupation as a gardener, or from some stranger they meet walking along a road or on a beach, or in some experience they might have behind the locked doors of an upper room.

The Teacher of these insights awaits them. He has come for an urgent visit and has already taken a seat in the waiting room.

Chapter 7

Wounded Healers

Aequanimitas

I served as an intern and resident on the Osler Medical Service of the Johns Hopkins Hospital. Hopkins is a place of great tradition. In fact, the man who served as Chief of Medicine when I was an intern, Dr. Victor McKusick, was more devoted to medical history and tradition than anyone I have ever known. Quite a few years before I arrived, McKusick had ordered that special neckties be produced for the department (he graciously allowed scarves for the women). The original design is still in use. To be honest, they are fairly ugly ties, modeled on the British public school ties: dark navy blue silk imprinted with a pattern of silver shields. Written on each shield is a Latin word that always invites inquiry from outsiders: *Aequanimitas* (equanimity).

This word was chosen for the Osler Medical Service Tie because it is the title of the most famous speech ever given by the first chief of medicine at the Johns Hopkins Hospital, Sir William Osler, M.D. Every intern was instructed to buy an Osler Tie and to wear it on Fridays. It has become its own tradition.

Now I wasn't yet a friar when I was an intern, and I didn't have much time to read the copy of Osler's famous speech that they gave me on the first day of internship, and I didn't much care for spending $20 for the tie. My salary, in 1982, was $14,000 for the year. Working 90 hours a week, that meant I was being paid a little less than $3 per hour. (I had participated in demonstrations and boycotts against California vineyard owners who had paid migrant farm workers that sort of money). In any event, I was derelict in my duty as an Osler intern. I never bought an Osler Tie.

In my own mind, I had justified this indiscretion in a most self-righteous fashion. I said to myself, all this talk of *Aequanimitas* represents an antiquated view of medicine. Such a Victorian, neo-Stoic emphasis on composure, the old British stiff upper lip, and repression of emotions represented the kind of medicine I was out to change. I was ready to elaborate on this defense pub-

111

licly if called upon to do so. But curiously, no one ever took notice of the fact that one of the Osler interns didn't have an Osler Tie.

Two years later, after having completed my initial training with the friars and having taken initial vows, I returned to Hopkins to start my residency. While I was away, Dr. McKusick had stepped down from his job as Chief to take over as Director of the Human Genome Project. A man named John Stobo, had taken over as William Osler Professor of Medicine and Chief of Medicine at the Johns Hopkins Hospital. During my first month back at Hopkins, I had to prepare the medical students to present to Dr. Stobo on Chief of Service Rounds—a big affair. I reviewed their case presentations, coached them on the pathophysiology, and rehearsed with them extensively. When they actually had their chance to present to Stobo, I was proud. I thought they had done a splendid job. But just as rounds were ending, Dr. Stobo took me aside and asked, "What's wrong, Dan?"

I turned red quickly. It was my first month back. I had barely known Stobo. I was rusty. I was nervous. I blurted out, "What do you mean, 'What's wrong?' What did I do?"

He said, "It's Friday. Where's your tie?"

All of my cool, carefully scripted, self-righteous arguments against *Aequanimitas* melted in a pool of sweat. "I...I don't own one," I said, rather meekly.

"Well, we'll fix that," he said. "Come with me."

I guess I had learned something about obedience from the friars. He took me to his office and gave me a tie. "Here," he said, winking. "Now wear this." I put it on, and walked out of the office.

To this day I wear my Osler Tie every Friday. In fact, I just got a new one a couple of months ago. They wear out after ten years. And over the years, I have learned to put aside my questions about *Aequanimit*as—not merely through obedience, but through understanding.

Osler didn't quite mean by the title of his famous speech what most casual observers think he meant. If one reads his speech carefully, one notes that he does talk of keeping calm in the face of adversity for the sake of the patient. And much of that is good. Patients don't want their physicians and nurses to turn into gelatin whenever they disclose bad news. Nor do they want physicians and nurses who are so flustered by circumstances in the hospital that they forget they're working there to serve the patients. But Osler was not prescribing the cold, aloof, detached, totally scientific attitude that characterizes too many contemporary clinicians. What he actually wrote was,

> Cultivate, then, gentlemen, such a judicious measure of obtuseness as will enable you to meet the exigencies of practice with firmness and courage, without, at the same time, hardening "the human heart by which we live."[1]

Today, Osler would understand that he would not be talking exclusively to gentlemen. But his sentiments are essentially correct. The equanimity he urged physicians and nurses to cultivate had more to do with the adequacy of their *attachment* to patients than with their *detachment*. He goes on to write,

> Curious, odd compounds are these fellow-creatures, at whose mercy you will be; full of fads and eccentricities, of whims and fancies; but the more closely we study their little foibles of one sort and another in the inner life which we see, the more surely is the conviction borne in upon us of the likeness of their weakness to our own. The similarity would be intolerable, if a happy egotism did not often render us forgetful of it. Hence the need of an ever-tender charity towards these fellow creatures...[2]

Osler's equanimity was more about avoiding the temptation to blame the patient than it was about maintaining one's distance from one's patients or preserving an icy coolness. This is interesting to reflect upon, because today there is an epidemic of blaming the patient. One hears frequent sneering remarks from health care professionals about "self-abusing patients." Many proposals for health care reform have included plans to tax cigarette smokers differentially because they are consuming valuable health care resources through their "sins." Independent of health care reform, one hears of self-righteous physicians refusing to care for cigarette smokers, drug abusers, and noncompliant patients. I often hear such arguments put forth quite strenuously by resident physicians during medical ethics classes, usually as they are stuffing cholesterol-rich pizza into their mouths. When I ask them whether I should withhold cardiac bypass surgery from them because of their own "sinful" consumption, I am only making Osler's point. The more closely we clinicians study our patients, the more striking becomes "the likeness of their weakness to our own."

Recognition of one's own foibles is a necessary ingredient in becoming a good clinician. The first stage in the process of becoming a wounded healer is recognizing that one is wounded and in need of healing oneself.

One of my fellow friars, a former missionary to Japan named Fr. Flavian Walsh, once said that there are three rules for becoming a good confessor: (1) be kind, (2) be kind, and (3) be kind. This may be why priests who are alcoholics in recovery often make such good confessors. They know human foibles, and they understand the likeness of the penitent's weakness to their own. Health care professionals would become far more effective if they were to pay more attention to the likeness between their patients' foibles and their own.

Failure

Osler also meant a bit more by *Aequanimitas* than putting up with the foibles of patients. He also reminds health care professionals:

> It is sad to think that, for some of you, there is in store disappointment, perhaps failure. You cannot hope, of course, to escape from the cares and anxieties incident to the professional life. Stand up bravely, even against the worst.[3]

Health care professionals are often far too convinced of their own perfection and of their own invulnerability. Doubtless, the system of training that physicians undergo helps to foster thoughts of invulnerability. But these thoughts are delusional. And delusional health care professionals are dangers to patients and dangers to themselves. Unless health care professionals are convinced of their own fallibility and vulnerability, they will either make serious mistakes or begin to take out their angers and frustrations upon patients, or both. The virtue of *Aequanimitas* can only be cultivated by healers who know their own wounded nature.

It is easy to understand how this delusion of perfection and invulnerability develops. Americans, in general, lead very privileged lives. This is especially true of physicians. Donald Nicholl has observed, however, how bad this can be.[4] He notes the curious paradox that perhaps the worst thing that could happen to anyone would be to have perfect health, never to have failed in any endeavor, and to have had all personal plans fulfilled, to be financially secure, to be warmly loved, and never to have suffered. Under such conditions, observes Nicholl, every one of us would become a monster. In fact, it is not precisely true of anyone. But the closer one's life comes to such conditions, the greater the danger of becoming a monster. And I'm sure that most health care professionals have known colleagues for whom this danger has become more reality than fiction.

I guess I am a rarity as a physician who does not play golf, but I think I now understand why so many physicians enjoy the sport. They certainly know better than to think that it is a great form of cardiovascular exercise. A colleague explained to me the popularity of golf among physicians several years ago.

I had just finished seeing a patient with a long slate of medical problems. He had cancer of the tongue and a good portion of his tongue had been removed. The surgeon was convinced that the cancer was completely gone, but he sent the patient to me because he was still smoking and also had high blood pressure. I had seen the patient only twice previously. In addition to the smoking and the blood pressure, he was also depressed. On this day, he returned to me, having taken the medications I had prescribed for his depression and for his blood pressure.

To my surprise, he looked like a new man. He told me he was sleeping again. He had not smoked a cigarette for two weeks. His blood pressure was normal. He reported a much improved mood. Needless to say, I was thrilled. I then proudly described this little clinical success story to my colleague and announced, "A cure!"

We are both internists. As internists, we are used to chronic incurable diseases, like arthritis, high blood pressure, diabetes, and AIDS. We are not used to cures. We are more used to dutifully urging people to change their lifestyles, usually without success. This clinical success story was, indeed, a rare event, and a genuine cause for celebration and justified pride. It was then that my colleague explained golf to me. He said, "You know, general internal medicine is a lot like golf. Most of the time you're just hacking around out there, but every once in a while you hit the ball perfectly and it gives you the encouragement to go on hacking around all the rest of the time." This colleague understood what *Aequanimitas* is all about. Wounded healers do far more hacking around out there on the fairway than they care to admit.

Mastery or Mystery?

The professional delusions of American medicine run deep. I remember an encounter with a postdoctoral fellow in oncology when I was an intern. One of our patients was dying—far beyond the possibility of cure or even of amelioration of the disease. She had leukemia. The last round of chemotherapy had wiped out all her normal bone marrow. All that had regenerated were leukemic white blood cells. She had no blood platelets to speak of. She was bleeding profusely. She had three different infections. She was in shock. Her kidneys had begun to fail. I had dutifully done all the "right" things designed to keep her alive. She was intubated, on a ventilator, on pressor drugs to keep her blood pressure up and her heart going. She was being transfused with red blood cells and blood platelets. She was on multiple antibiotics. She was receiving temporary dialysis.

I really didn't know why we were persisting in her treatment, and I remember just feeling awful. It felt even worse when I was congratulated for having done such a good job keeping her alive. I felt that everything that I had done had been more destructive than constructive. I had been up all night and was exhausted. They let me go home early that day. And as I was leaving, the fellow said to me, "Don't worry. I'll be able to keep her alive until the morning. I just love it when patients are like this. When all the tubes are in place, I'm in complete control. I control her blood pressure; I control her breathing; I control how much fluid goes in; I control how much fluid goes out. And they can't talk back. Gosh, I wish they were all like this."

I was horrified. Sure enough, she was alive when I returned the next morning. But by noon, we stopped paying attention to the dials. Our little game was over. She died that afternoon. Presumably, we had allowed her to die only after the fellow had lost interest in exercising complete control over her body solely for the sake of control.

There is probably an element of this in all health care professionals, whether ICU nurse, pulmonologist, oncologist, or family physician. It may not be expressed so matter-of-factly, but many health care professionals are driven by an intense desire for control. At least the people who make up the drug advertisements believe this is so, even if health care professionals would deny it. I recently cut out an advertisement for a brand name anti-coagulant a few months ago that appealed specifically to this desire. The advertisement claimed that because there was uniform bioavailability and predictable absorption of their brand of the drug, one could control the thinning of the blood more precisely. This was touted as its real advantage over all the generic brands. The advertisement ended by announcing in grand, bold letters the precise sentiments to which it was appealing— CONTROL! MASTERY!

It has been my observation that sometimes an intense desire to control the events and people around them in their private lives spills over into the professional lives of clinicians, even taking hold of their interactions with patients. Sometimes their intense desire to control everything there is about patients and the delivery of health care spills over into the rest of their lives, even their interactions with their own families. However it gets started, health care professionals need to recognize it as a severe source of dysfunction for some of them, and as at least a temptation for the rest of them. *Their* desires, *their* plans, and *their* choices are not the central organizing principles of the universe! And for those of us who are Christians, it must be admitted that even our faith is not the central organizing principle of the universe. It is the God in whom we place our faith who is the central organizing principle of the universe. God says, "It was not you who chose me, it was I who chose you" (Jn. 15:16).

To paraphrase the philosopher, Gabriel Marcel, a patient is not a problem to be solved, but a mystery in whose presence the clinician is privileged to dwell. "A problem is something which I meet, which I find complete before me, but which I can therefore lay siege to and reduce. But a mystery is something in which I myself am involved, and it can therefore only be thought of as a sphere in which the distinction between what is in me and what is before me loses its meaning and its initial validity."[5] From this perspective, the practice of making medicine into a science of engineering is the most thoroughly dehumanizing stance one can take toward a patient. Conceiving of the patient merely as an object to be scientifically manipulated, essentially no different from a tadpole in a dish, undermines the meaning of healing by denying the mystery of the clinician-patient relationship.

The attitude reflected in the conception of the patient as a problem is pervasive in modern medicine. I control the breathing; I control the blood pressure; I control the temperature, the heart rate, the level of the blood thinner. If there's a problem to be fixed, I'll fix it. If it can't be fixed, I'll get rid of it and find a new one. What's the mystery?

But while such thinking seems grotesque and alien in one sense, I suspect it sounds very familiar in another sense. Medicine is fast becoming *industrialized.* Patients are becoming items on a conveyor belt. If genetic defects are discovered and can't be fixed, we simply discard them. If they get old and worn down, we throw them away. We just have different names for these practices so they don't sound so heinous. We prefer to call these practices total quality management, preventive prenatal genetics, and physician-assisted death.

The moral theologian Paul Ramsey thought that this depersonalization was the central problem in contemporary ethics and medicine. He wrote a whole book entitled, *The Patient as Person.*[6] We have yet to heed his warning. Ramsey understood that while medicine is deeply human, it is at the same time utterly transcendental. Medicine's struggle for absolute control is an impossible task. One cannot control the most important things about being human. For example, one cannot choose one's own biological parents or alter the fact that everyone will die. Yet medicine is about both birth and death. Medicine is about the universal need of all human beings for healing and about the fact that no human being can provide the ultimate healing that all of us need. Human beings are created in the image and the likeness of the Creator. To treat a patient is to have an encounter with the Holy Mystery of God. As such, human beings are endowed with a dignity that cannot be taken from them. It is certainly true that human dignity can be ignored, trampled upon, or abused; but it cannot be eradicated by sinful deeds or natural misfortune. To treat patients as machines over which we have complete control is both folly and sin.

Being in the Right Place

These are troubled and uncertain times for health care professionals. But it is instructive to note that such were the times in which Jesus lived as well. To be a Jew living in Palestine under Roman occupation two thousand years ago was to live in times of uncertainty, doubt, suffering, change, and social upheaval. It was to the people who lived in that historical situation that Jesus said, Blessed are the poor in spirit, the sorrowing, the meek, those who hunger and thirst for righteousness, the merciful, the clean of heart, the peacemakers, and those persecuted for the sake of righteousness (Mt 5:3-10).

I am told that the "blessed are you when..." formulation of the Beatitudes is more literally (and not less interestingly) translated as "you are in the right place when..." In the face of the present turmoil in health care, I hear tales of many physicians who are retiring early, quitting, or getting jobs as HMO executives or entrepreneurs. I hear tales of many nurses going to get MBAs or getting jobs as utilization reviewers for HMOs. Now, I know perfectly well that there may be very good reasons for doing these things, like needing a job after having been laid off or needing to arrange for hours that are more manageable for raising a family. But it pains me to think that many are seeking these jobs because they can't stomach what's happening to their professions. I do not deny that times are tough and that obstacles are continually being placed in the way of health care professionals who really care about patients. But what will happen if the all the good ones quit? Will health care be stuck only with the bad apples? Or can those who have the more admirable attitudes learn somehow to persist in spite of all the bureaucratic barriers, financial incentives, demands to spend less time with patients, and all the rest. Can health care professionals understand that somehow, even in the midst of all of this, they are "in the right place"? All health care workers are called to find holiness in the here-and-now, day-in-and-day-out, pain-in-the-butt practices of medicine, nursing, and the allied health professions precisely in these very troubled times. To continue to care for the sick while still maintaining equanimity, compassion, humility, a zeal for justice, a sense of mercy, a clean heart, and a spirit of reconciliation, despite all the persecutorial patterns that the government and the third-party payers can muster, is to live the Beatitudes in health care.

Grace

On the other hand, any health care professional who begins to think that he or she can "do it all" courts unmitigated spiritual disaster. This is the greatest temptation for those who really do care—to think that it all falls on their shoulders. But the sheer mass of the world's sickness is far bigger than any physician or nurse. There is no such thing as Superman or Superwoman. The sociological crucibles from which the modern plagues emerge— injection drug use and AIDS in the inner city; and cocaine, alcohol, and inflammatory bowel disease on Wall Street—are quite beyond the reach of health care per se. No individual can possibly fix all these problems; and until they are fixed, the epidemics will persist. So the epidemics do persist. But like Dr. Rieux, in Camus' *The Plague*, physicians and nurses have a choice. They can either flee or stay at their stations and do whatever they can do. No more can be asked of them. No less will be required of them. And in this experience, perhaps, they will come to the insight of Fr. Paneloux, who tells Dr. Rieux that in the experience of living through the city's plague, he has finally discovered the meaning of grace.[7]

Grace comes in the midst of the stuff of life. It comes in our struggles and in our triumphs, in our daily attention to what is ours to do in the midst of our hopeless inadequacy. Understanding what grace means is a lifetime's work. It is on his deathbed that the curé in *The Diary of a Country Priest* comes to the recognition that "Grace is everywhere."[8]

But while grace saves even those who are naive enough to think that there is nothing from which they need to be saved, we also know of those who find it all too burdensome. Some driven by pride, or greed, or parental expectations that don't fit their talents and personalities, are racked by cynical bitterness even before they come to the healing professions. Others try to be Superman or Superwoman and burn out. Health care professionals need to be attentive to signs of burn-out in themselves and in their colleagues. And they need to be quick to intervene before it is too late. There is almost nothing worse than a bitter, cynical physician or nurse.

Pastoral care teams in hospitals are often very helpful in this regard. If they are doing their jobs right, much of their work will consist of caring for the wounded healers who work in the hospital or medical center. I find myself, too, since I am known to be a friar more by the staff than by patients, frequently called upon to minister to the needs of staff. And their needs are many.

But I do not wish to imply that these themes are relevant only for those health care professionals who are burned out. Even that majority who are managing to cope with the stresses of their work still need to acknowledge their wounds and look for healing and strength for themselves. Sometimes prayer and the listening ear of a spouse are enough. Others may find some consolation in discussion groups—even in such things as medical humanities reading groups. All physicians and nurses make mistakes. All fail. All have feelings of guilt that need to be dealt with. Almost all physicians have been or will be sued and will know the pain, doubt, and isolation that this brings. Physicians, especially, seem to get early reinforcement from the health care educational system for simply suppressing their feelings when things go wrong in the care of patients. This is a distorted view of *Aequanimitas.* Health care professionals need to acknowledge these feelings of failure, inadequacy, guilt, and of being overwhelmed by the sheer mass of patients' needs. To suppress these feelings invites the danger of becoming unfeeling. Many need to unburden themselves. Some may even need counseling.

I personally bring my thoughts and feelings about adverse events to the sacrament of reconciliation. I start out by saying that I know in my head that whatever happened is not a sin. I assure my confessor that I am not plagued by recurrent thoughts of hell. I explain that I did no intentional harm. But I need somehow to acknowledge, ritually, that bad things happened and I got mixed up in them. Something was done or not done that could have been handled better. A patient was hurt or even died. I bear some responsibility for this. I feel awful about it all. I need to be forgiven.

What drives me to conduct myself in such a fashion is that in the last analysis, reconciliation means that I acknowledge my need to confess my humanity to God. Bless me, Father, I am a frail human being. I need to be reminded of God's love for me, a wounded healer who isn't exactly perfect (despite what his patients seem to think). I need to hear words of reconciliation and peace. I am threatened, in a radical sense, by my inadequacy to the task of healing. And I need to be saved from this.

My spiritual director and confessor, who knows very little about medicine, listens to all these musings of mine. He is patient and kind. He usually says a few words to me about the cross, and about being sure that I am not too hard on myself. Through his prayers, I am reconciled to God sacramentally. And my frank admission of my nature as a wounded, fallible creature, much less than a medical deity, becomes a moment of grace. And I get on with it.

Grace is everywhere. Here and now. In the stuff of it.

I santi

I once bought an Italian version of St. Bonaventure's *Life of St. Francis* for one of our older friars who had worked for many years as a confessor at the Church of St. John Lateran in Rome. I vividly remember the dust jacket. The headline of the description of the book said, in Italian, *I santi non sono i meno diffetosi ma i più corragiosi* (The holy are not the least defective, but the most courageous).

Holiness is not about being perfect. It is about the courage to acknowledge imperfection. It is about the courage to act in the face of imperfection. It is about the courage to be less than super-human and yet more than the irredeemable, dismal, rational maximizer of self-interest that some philosophers and some economists say represents the reality of all that human beings can ever be.

It is the call to this kind of holiness that I want to urge upon health care professionals today. To be a wounded healer is to be this kind of doctor or nurse. Holy, not by virtue of any saccharine practices or hypocritical pretensions of perfection. But holy by virtue of honesty. Holy by virtue of courage. Here. Now. In the stuff of it.

Those of us who work in health care institutions and call our-selves Christians are capable of such holiness. We doubtless have trouble seeing it around us, or even seeing the potential in our-selves. But we are called to holiness. We have only first to recog-nize that we ourselves are wounded. To quote the gospel of Luke, the physician-evangelist, "Physician, heal yourself" (Lk. 4:23). For until we recognize that we are in need of healing ourselves and recognize in the weakness of our patients a weakness not unlike our own, we will never be very good healers.

Epilogue:
The Joy of Practice

Joy is an awkward word in our society. It gets trotted out only at Christmas time and then put back in the attic with the rest of the decorations to wait for another year. Joy seems an even more awkward word in health care. In the face of sickness, death, and so much suffering, how could anyone talk about joy?

On my general internal medicine consultation rounds, I occasionally used to be called to the oncology ward. Quite often, when I arrived on the ward, I would find the nurses there laughing together in the medication room or at the ward desk. They seemed to be exuberantly joyful. To tease them, I would often say with mock sternness, "Stop laughing! Don't you know that cancer is a very serious business?" Of course, I would elicit the response for which I was looking. They would start laughing even harder at the absurdity of the question.

These nurses were good nurses. They were not making light of what they were doing. They worked hard and cared deeply about their patients. They were not cynically making fun of them. They were not acting out the bitter laughter of *The House of God*,[1] nor was their humor the black humor that is sometimes found in medical institutions and hypothesized to be a way of coping with pain, sickness, fear, suffering, and death. Their laughter was not a form of denial. Their humor was genuinely joyful. Their joy was about being human. Their humor was about the human predicament. Their laughter was about the pretentiousness and the foibles and the contradictions and the absurdities that the nurses knew they shared with their patients. Theirs was the humor of *Aequanimitas*. The patients laughed as well. It is true that laughter is medicine.

Despite all the rampant cynicism, bitterness, and aloofness that one sees in modern health care, joy is possible. One *can* be happy in health care. Christians *ought* to be happy in health care. Good healers are joyful people. Their joy is contagious.

Joy comes with satisfaction. It comes with self-knowledge.

Health care professionals who know that they are loved by God are satisfied and know who they really are. They can see beyond the horizon of sickness and death into the marvelous light promised by God. They know what God promises for their patients as well as what God promises for them.

In saying this, I am not advocating an absurd, other-worldly, pietistic, sugar-coated joy. A health care professional with a spirituality based on such a notion of joy would not make it through the ravages of the first night shift in which a patient suffers and dies. The joy I am invoking is not the antonym of suffering. One can recognize one's finitude and still be joyful. In fact, it can be stated securely that one cannot be genuinely joyful unless one *has* come to terms with one's finitude. The joy I am invoking has been described by the Nobel prize winning poet Rabindranath Tagore as

> ...the joy that sets the twin brothers, life and death, dancing over the wide world, the joy that sweeps in with the tempest, shaking and waking all life with laughter, the joy that sits still with its tears on the open red lotus of pain, and the joy that throws everything it has upon the dust, and knows not a word.[2]

Such joy is possible only for people who are dwelling in the present, not in a promise about the future. Such joy comes from a secure knowledge that the kingdom of God is at hand.

Joy is only possible for persons who are attentive to the present. One cannot be happy if one is continually ruminating about what might have been or fretting over what one wishes will come to pass. Americans have a tough time with real joy. Americans are oriented toward outcomes, expectations, and the future; toward ever more competition in proving that they deliver the best results, and anxiously pondering how things might have turned out if only they had chosen differently. This makes it hard to be happy. In health care, these tendencies are exaggerated. Worries about what will happen next to the patient and worries about their own future careers blot out the possibility of joy for many health care professionals. Joy is a present tense phenomenon. It is possible only if one attends to the moment.

Gratitude has been called the heart of prayer.[3] It is also the heart of joy. Only health care professionals who are grateful can be joyful. To be joyful is to be attentive to the profound meaning of the privilege of serving the sick and to be grateful for that privilege. To be joyful is to be fascinated by people—in all colors, shapes, and sizes; of all sorts of temperaments; from all social strata—and to be conscious of how wonderful it is that God made them all and grateful that one has had the chance to meet so many on such intimate terms. To be joyful is to note the regenerative mysteries of the body, to understand something of how it all works, and to be grateful that one has been given the opportunity to nudge along the process of healing. To be joyful is to know that one has been gifted with hands and with a mind through which the healing power of the Spirit can be mediated and to be grateful for those gifts. To be joyful is to pour out the wine of fervent zeal and the oil of compassion day in and day out and to be grateful that the source of these liquors is inexhaustible.

The secret joy of health care is people. If doctors, nurses, social workers, technicians, and their colleagues can just remember that every single patient is a gift from God, they will understand that they have been richly blessed. They will be very joyful people, for "good measure, packed together, shaken down, and overflowing, will be poured into your lap."(Lk. 6:38). The meaning of Samaritanism is compassion, and compassion is true joy.

Notes

1. Spirituality and the Health Care Professional

1. Sigmund Freud, *Civilization and Its Discontents,* trans. James Strachey (New York: W. W. Norton, 1961), 21–32.
2. Shusaku Endo, *Deep River,* trans. Van C. Gessl (New York: New Directions Books, 1994).
3. Karl Rahner, S.J., *Foundations of Christian Faith* (New York: Seabury Press, 1978), 44–51.
4. T. S. Eliot, "The Dry Salvages," II, in *Four Quartets* (New York: Harcourt, Brace, and World, 1971), 39.
5. Daniel P. Sulmasy, O.F.M., "*Exousia:* Healing with Authority in the Christian Tradition," in *Theological Analyses of the Clinical Encounter,* eds. Gerald P. McKenney and Jonathan R. Sande (Dordrecht, Netherlands: Kluwer, 1994), 85–107.
6. Warfield T. Longcope, "Methods and Medicine," *Bulletin of the Johns Hopkins Hospital* 50 (1940): 4–20.
7. St. Clare, "Second Letter to Blessed Agnes of Prague," in *The Writings of Francis and Clare,* trans. Regis J. Armstrong, O.F.M., Cap. and Ignatius C. Brady, O.F.M. (New York: Paulist Press, 1982), 196.

2. Medicine, Love and the Art of Being Uncertain

1. T.S. Eliot, "The Love Song of J. Alfred Prufrock," in T.S. Eliot: The *Complete Poems and Plays* (New York: Harcourt, Brace, Jovanovitch, 1971), 3–7.
2. Evelyn C.Y. Chan and Daniel P. Sulmasy, "What Should Men Know

Before Giving Consent for Prostate Specific Antigen Screening?" *The Journal of General Internal Medicine* ll, Suppl. 1 (1996): 114.

3. James Dickey, *Deliverance* (Boston: Houghton Mifflin, 1970).

4. T.S. Eliot, "The Wasteland," in *Complete Poems and Plays,* 49.

5. Jean M. Mitchell and Jonathan H. Sunshine, "Consequences of Physicians' Ownership of Health Care Facilities–Joint Ventures in Radiation Therapy," *New England Journal of Medicine* 327 (1992): 1497–1501.

6. Eve A. Kerr, Brian S. Mittman, Ron D. Hays, Albert L. Siu, Barbara Leake, and Robert H. Brook, "Managed Care and Capitation in California: How Do Physicians at Financial Risk Control Their Own Utilization?" *Annals of Internal Medicine* 123 (1995): 500–504.

7. A.J. Ayer, *Language, Truth, and Logic* (New York: Dover, 1952), 5–26.

8. Ludwig Wittgenstein, *Tractatus Logicus-Philosophicus,* 2.1-2.225, trans. C.K. Ogden (London: Routledge, 1990), 38–43.

9. Jerome P. Kassirer, "Images in Medicine," *New England Journal of Medicine* 326 (1992), 829–30.

10. Bernard J.F. Lonergan, *Insight: A Study in Human Understanding* (San Francisco: Harper and Row, 1978), 110.

11. William Osler, *Aphorisms from His Bedside Teachings and Writings,* No. 265, ed. William B. Bean (New York: Henry Schuman, 1950), 125.

12. Lao Tsu, *The Tao Te Ching,* No. 71., trans. Gia-Fu Feng and Jane English (New York: Vintage Books), 1972.

13. T. S. Eliot, "The *Pensees of Pascal*," in *Selected Essays* (New York: Harcourt, Brace, and Co., 1950), 363.

14. Paul Ramsey, as quoted in Courtney S. Campbell, "Religion and Moral Meaning in Bioethics," *Hastings Center Report* 20, suppl. (July/August, 1990): 4–10.

15. Edmund D. Pellegrino and David C. Thomasma, *A Philosophical Basis of Medical Practice* (New York: Oxford University Press, 1981), 139, 276.

16. Letter to James H. Forest, Feb. 21, 1966, in *The Hidden Ground of Love: The Letters of Thomas Merton on Religious Experience and Social Concern,* ed. William H. Shannon (New York: Farrar-Strauss-Giroux, 1985), 294–7.

3. The Wine of Fervent Zeal and the Oil of Compassion

1. C.E. Lewis, D.M. Prout, E.P. Chalmers, and B. Leake "How satisfying is the practice of internal medicine? A national survey," *Annals of Internal Medicine* 114 (1991):1-5.

2. St. Bonaventure, *The Virtues of a Religious Superior (De sex alis*

seraphim), trans. Sabinus Mollitor, O.F.M. (St. Louis: B. Herder, 1920), 30.

3. H. R. Niebuhr, *Christ and Culture* (New York: Harper and Row, 1951).

4. William Osler, "On the need of a radical reform in our methods of teaching medical students." *Medical News* 82 (1903):49–53.

5. Nikos Kazantzakis, *Saint Francis,* trans. P.A. Bien (New York: Simon and Schuster, 1962), 94–96; Thomas of Celano, "The Second Life of Francis," 9, in *St Francis of Assisi, Writings and Early Biographies: English Sources for the Life of St. Francis,* ed. M.A. Habig (Chicago: Franciscan Herald Press, 1973), 369.

6. T.S. Eliot, "East Coker" IV, *Four Quartets,* in *T.S. Eliot: The Complete Poems and Plays* (New York: Harcourt, Brace, Jovanovich, 1971), 127.

7. St. Bonaventure, *The Virtues of a Religious Superior (De sex alis seraphim),* trans. Sabinus Mollitor, O.F.M. (St. Louis: B. Herder, 1920), 33.

8. Henri Nouwen, *The Wounded Healer* (Garden City, N.Y.: Doubleday, 1972), 90.

9. William Osler, *"Aequanimitas,"* in *Aequanimitas, With Other Addresses to Physicians, Nurses, and Other Practitioners of Medicine,* 3rd. ed. (Philadelphia: Blakiston, 1932), 1–11.

10. T. Mizrahi, *Getting Rid of Patients* (New Brunswick, N.J.: Rutgers University Press, 1986).

11. Nouwen, 91–96.

12. Thomas of Celano, "The First Life of St. Francis," 3–5, in *St. Francis of Assisi, Writings and Early Biographies: English Sources,* 231–35.

13. *The Autobiography of St. Ignatius of Loyola,* trans J.F. O'Callaghan, ed. J.C. Olin (New York: Harper and Row, 1974), 21–26.

4. God-Talk at the Bedside

1. Dale A. Matthews, *The Faith Factor: An Annotated Bibliography of Clinical Research on Spiritual Subjects* (Arlington, Virginia: National Institute for Health Care Research, 1993).

2. Daniel P. Sulmasy, Gail Geller, David M. Levine, and Ruth R. Faden, "The Quality of Mercy: Caring for Patients With 'Do Not Resuscitate' Orders," *Journal of the American Medical Association* 267 (1992): 682–86.

3. Edmund D. Pellegrino and David C. Thomasma. *For the Patient's Good: The Restoration of Beneficence in Health Care* (New York: Oxford University Press, 1987).

4. "The Testament," in *Francis and Clare: The Complete Works.* Trans.

Regis J. Armstrong, O.F.M., Cap. and Ignatius C. Brady, O.F.M. (New York: Paulist Press, 1982), 153–56.

5. Prayer and the Five Senses: A Physician's Meditation

1. Karl Rahner, *On Prayer* (New York: Paulist Press, 1968), 9.
2. "Letter to the Entire Order," 29, in *Francis and Clare: The Complete Works,* trans. Regis J. Armstrong, O.F.M., Cap. and Ignatius C. Brady, O.F.M. (New York: Paulist Press, 1982), 58.
3. St. Bonaventure, "The Soul's Journey Into God," II.1, in *Bonaventure,* trans. Ewert Cousins (New York: Paulist Press, 1978), 69.
4. T.S. Eliot, "Ash Wednesday," in *Selected Poems* (New York: Harcourt, Brace, and World, 1936), 92.
5. Pablo Neruda, "The great tablecloth," in *Extravagaria,* trans. Alastair Reid (London: Jonathan Cape, 1972), 44–47.
6. St. John of the Cross, "The Dark Night," in *The Collected Works of St. John of the Cross,* trans. Kieran Kavanaugh, O.C.D. and Otilio Rodriguez, O.C.D. (Washington, D.C.: Institute of Carmelite Studies, 1979), 293–384.
7. St. Francis of Assisi, "Admonitions," XIX, in *Francis and Clare,* 33.
8. T.S. Eliot, "East Coker," III. In *Four Quartets* (New York: Harcourt, Brace, and World, 1971), 28.
9. Bonaventure, "The Soul's Journey Into God," II.12, 76.
10. Howard B. Beckman and Richard M. Frankel, "The Effect of Physician Behavior on the Collection of Data," *Annals of Internal Medicine* 101 (1984): 692–96.
11. Richard Baron, "An Introduction to Medical Phenomenology: I Can't Hear You While I'm Listening," *Annals of Internal Medicine* 103 (1985): 606–11.
12. Ezra Pound, "The Garden," in *Norton Anthology of Poetry,* ed., Arthur M. Eastman (New York: W.W. Norton, 1970), 979.

6. Suffering, Spirituality, and Health Care

1. H.P. Greenwald, "Interethnic Differences in Pain Perception," *Pain* 44 (1991), 157–63.
2. John Paul II, *"Salvifici Doloris,"* Origins 13 (Feb. 23, 1984), 609–24.
3. Eric J. Cassell, *The Nature of Suffering and the Goals of Medicine* (New York: Oxford University Press, 1991), 37–43.
4. John Donne, Meditation No. 17, "Now, this Bell tolling softly for another, saies to me, Thou must die," in *Devotions Upon Emergent Occasions,* ed. Anthony Raspa (Montreal and London: McGill-Queen's University Press, 1975), 86–90.

5. Thomas Hobbes, *Leviathan,* 42, ed. Richard Tuck (Cambridge, UK: Cambridge University Press, 1991), 63.

6. Warren T. Reich, "Speaking of Suffering: A Moral Account of Compassion," *Soundings* 72 (1989), 83–108.

7. John Hick, *Evil and the God of Love* (London: MacMilllan, 1966), 340–45.

8. John Paul II, *Salvifici Doloris* 23.

9. Vaclav Havel, *Disturbing the Peace* (New York: Vintage Books, 1991), 181.

7. Wounded Healers

1. William Osler, *"Aequanimitas,"* in *Aequanimitas, With Other Addresses to Medical Students, Nurses, and Practitioners of Medicine,* 3rd ed. (New York: McGraw-Hill, 1906), 5.

2. Osler, *Aequanimitas,* 6.

3. Osler, *Aequanimitas,* 7–8.

4. Donald Nicholl, *Holiness* (New York: Paulist Press, 1987), 145–46.

5. Gabriel Marcel, *Being and Having,* trans. Katherine Farrer (Glasgow, The University Press, 1949), 117.

6. Paul Ramsey, *The Patient as Person* (New Haven, Conn.: Yale University Press, 1970).

7. Albert Camus, *The Plague,* trans. Stuart Gilbert (New York: Vintage, 1991), 219.

8. Georges Bernanos, *The Diary of a Country Priest,* trans. Pamela Morris (New York: Carroll and Graf, 1984), 298.

Epilogue: The Joy of Practice

1. Samuel Shem, *The House of God: A Novel* (New York: R Marek, 1978).

2. Rabindranath Tagore, *Gitanjali,* No. 58 (London: Macmillan, 1953), 53.

3. David Steindl-Rast, *Gratefulness: The Heart of Prayer* (New York: Paulist Press, 1992).